the
caring
city
HEALTH, ECONOMY
AND ENVIRONMENT

Izaskun Chinchilla

For Roberto and Lope Marín, and for my mother.

TABLE OF CONTENTS

Part One

Exposed to the Elements

CHAPTER 1 THE DIMENSIONS OF THE CITY AND ITS INHABITANTS

Exposed to the elements

It's common practice among essayists to open with dictionary definitions or with explanations of the etymological origins of terms that will be important to the development of their argument. The literature on architecture or urban design is no exception. I think a good way to introduce the reader to the tone of this book is to begin, precisely, by talking about what tends to be left out of a definition in the dictionary or an etymological explanation. Specifically, I've chosen the word "elements" to talk about what is missing from the institutional definitions of words.

The definition of the word "elements" in Webster's dictionary reads merely that its use as a noun refers to "weather conditions, especially: violent or severe weather" and that it is often used in the phrase "exposed to the elements". The etymological explanations tell us that "element" comes from the Latin *elementum*, referring to "a first principle", or "earth, air, fire, or water; one of the four things regarded by the ancients as the constituents of all things".

These definitions leave out an endless number of connotations. Imagine a woman who is planning a risky trip, which she has been forced to put together at the last minute or in a rush, without enough time for preparations. If at some point she thinks about the word *elements* the night before she leaves, the associations with inclement weather, being outdoors, and being subject to outside temperatures would only be minor, limited aspects among the overall reactions that would be elicited by the term. The official definitions or the etymology would seem like a trifle compared to the internal defenselessness evoked by hearing, or even just thinking about, "the elements" when you're already feeling anxious or uncertain about the immediate future. In the mind of the woman about to set off on her trip, the term "the elements" will conjure any number of images. There will probably be lightning, thunder, wind, dark clouds, maybe even snow. Additionally, it's likely she will imagine feeling chilled to the bone, feeling tired, afraid of being attacked, of being alone, of losing her belongings, feeling sleepless and forced to be on the alert. The most intense sensations evoked by the word are the ones associated with how our bodies react, but those aren't included in the dictionary definition, and etymologists don't study them.

The official or institutional information about things is wholly inadequate when it comes to describing a subject's feelings or experiences. You can spend seven years studying architecture and still have very little ability to imagine what your day-to-day life as a practitioner will be like, and even less ability to predict how acting in the role of architect will make you feel. Job contracts presage very little about the real practice required in executing them; meeting minutes are often disappointing for people who were actually present, and traffic accident reports include only the smallest fraction of the overall experiences of the people involved.

From the One-Dimensional Man to the Multi-Dimensional City

Having rediscovered Herbert Marcuse's *One-dimensional Man*, I understand better why I find these definitions to be so incomplete. Marcuse, drawing on Freud, argues that the concept of reality is built on an important biological foundation. Both men assert that we construct our image of our surroundings with an acceptance of the limitations imposed upon us by our environment. In other words, they claim that a human being's behavior is intuitive *a priori*, and that we construct our definition of reality by interiorizing the difficulties that the world around us causes to our biological or instinctive functions. Given this construction, the mechanisms of attention, memory and reason serve to reorganize our instincts. Reality, therefore, has not only a biological foundation (because we have constructed it in an attempt to satisfy our instincts), but also a subjective and multidimensional foundation, because these episodes of attention, memory and reason are different for everyone, and they are strung together and organized hierarchically in different ways by each individual. The word "elements" will evoke physical sensations in each of us, organized – as we saw earlier – through attention, memory, and reason.

The biological foundations of the concept of reality and its multidimensional aspects, different for each person, are lost when culture institutionalizes that idea of reality. Experience becomes conditioned by ways of speaking and expressing concepts that are formulated by the organization of society; they carry a predefined semantic weight, which prevents us from thinking, analyzing or delving into them freely. The meaning of the message isn't formed or constructed, it is only used, because it has been predefined.

Marcuse speaks out against the encyclopedic, enlightenment-era, positivist transformation of a reality in which things are characterized by having a single dimension and are independent of the subject that experiences them, perceives them and is exposed to them. Precisely this is the source of my grievance: the strongest associations awakened by the word "elements" are cold, discomfort, or the inability to fall asleep when you're afraid, for example, that someone might steal your laptop if you do. They are multi-dimensional and biological sensations.

According to Marcuse, aside from the repression of the biological dimension of human beings, many of the institutions that "represent" us and organize our lives are guided by the *performance principle* (Marcuse, 2014). He argues that the culture of productivity has turned human beings into slaves of work to such an extent that we understand things, objects, spaces, and events in keeping with their role in the productive sector. Vehicles are means of transportation, citizens are employees or freelancers, and the environment has become a series of natural resources. That is why, according to the dictionary, what we need to know about the word *elements* is what makes sure a farm worker can interpret the sign "Do not leave the equipment exposed to the elements." The connotations of feelings of numbness, insomnia, and risk associated with the word don't correlate as directly to a performance principle in the working world, and, therefore, they are deserving of less attention on the part of institutional culture. In our culture, the names we give to things have taken on a practical dimension, intended to make sure the people who work with those "things" can understand which behaviors are appropriate.

Institutions take away, in part, the full experience of our surroundings. They turn it into something impersonal, abstract, that doesn't have a relationship with our bodies. But, at the same time, they don't deprive us all equally. Because institutional definitions are oriented toward the performance principle, they are much more akin to perceptions, much more precise and complete, when it comes the people who have traditionally participated in the world of work –

adult men – and they fail to account for the perspectives of children, women, or the elderly.

Our institutions fill our environments with signs like "Do not leave the equipment exposed to the elements." Does a man of working age, an elderly man, a young girl, or a 90-pound woman feel alluded to equally upon reading that sign? Children and the elderly aren't likely to feel the sign is speaking to them, since it is addressed to citizens who are expected to act. The 90-pound woman is likely to look at it with a certain annoyance and mutter something like "if it's possible". Our perceptions of reality are different depending on our bodies, our previous experience, and many other factors. What institutions end up doing, de facto, under the guise of objectivity, is focusing their messages on a small part of the population whose capabilities are assumed to be uniform.

The institutions involved in working with the city have also robbed us of its biological and multidimensional meaning. Take, for example, the guiding principles of 20th-century urban planning: zoning or the organization of circulations. Both are tools informed by the performance principle. Zoning determines which uses can take place in each area of the city, but those "uses" don't include sunbathing or walking. The uses stipulated by the aforementioned tool are residential, institutional, or industrial. Those are convenient descriptions for an investor when it comes to deciding whether a purchase of land will be profitable. The management of circulations, on the other hand, pursues efficiency in transportation, fundamentally of goods and workers.

Being a woman, being a mother, being ill, having restricted mobility, or being a dependent person means that the messages guided by the performance principle don't seem to apply. And as a result, the definitions given by the dictionary, or by the city we live in, may seem like foreign realities, divorced from our expectations and disconnected from our experiences. Marcuse was not referring specifically to mothers, people with the flu, or dependent people, but he did associate women with the perspective of "creative receptivity" (Marcuse, n.d.) – i.e., the ability to perceive what is possible as more real than what leads to immediate action. To use Marcuse's own terms, women are less affected by the performance principle, which is just one way of understanding reality, governed by "efficiency and prowess in the fulfillment of competitive economic and acquisitive functions". We would maintain that women also have a greater capacity to act under the "reality principle", which Marcuse defines as "the sum total of the norms and values which govern behavior in an established society, embodied in its institutions, relationships, etc." Although Marcuse never said it, he might well have assumed that it wouldn't have made sense to write *The One-Dimensional Woman*, since, despite the effects industrialization, women maintain a concept of reality that is less guided by practical, effective action aimed at productivity.

To take this idea even further, women not only maintain multidimensionality as individuals, but as a collective. And, with other authors,[1] I support this assertion, making a reflection that is, in a way, parallel to that of Marcuse. If the market has made men one-dimensional because it channels their understanding of reality toward the satisfaction of mercantile pursuits, women have maintained their multidimensional understanding of reality in part because much of their labor is given away for free; the things entrusted to women aren't associated with a market value. Not only do we take care of others without expecting financial compensation, but we do it, or hope to do it, without intervention on the part of institutional regulation (Still, 1997). Feminine culture has its

1 For example, Judith Still, author of *Feminine Economies*, argues that women's perception of the universe is conditioned by the fact that their work is offered free of charge and is not governed by market laws. Nancy Chodorow explains how the construction of female identity takes place through the establishment of relationships or connections.

own values, which, for the time being, are still somewhat more independent of the objective of efficiency or productivity. As I see it, there is no doubt that one of the things that has saved us from the performance principle ruling completely over our understanding is that we are still, for the most part, the ones in charge of care. In the world of care, caresses, fears, bodies, physical sensations, and the ghosts of things that are useless in the eyes of the working world, but which can terrify us or enliven our spirits, constitute the true basis of our forms of socialization and the foundations of our most meaningful relationships.

I think it is worth asking, while trying to avoid a hasty reading of gender, whether those who have designed, managed and governed our cities have failed to incorporate the other dimensions that we have highlighted here and which the dictionary definitions ignore, and whether the performance principle has been foremost in their understanding of reality. Such cities might understand public space, for example, as the space that helps us get from home to work, without considering whether, for some, the street is synonymous with relationships and coming together, while for others it signifies exposure or risk. And, of course, without considering whether there are circumstances that will make it more likely for human beings' subjective perceptions to be altered. Furthermore, it is worth asking whether there are – or whether there could be – cities, or fragments of them, that have been shaped by the principle of a multidimensional reality and imagining what advantages they would offer. I'd like to dedicate the next chapter to doing just that.

CHAPTER 2 A SAFE ROUTE TO SCHOOL.
THE BIKING TO SCHOOL PROJECT (LONDON)

Participation, Engagement and Distributed Knowledge

To reflect on the different dimensions of the city and a holistic vision of them, I will introduce a specific example that offers me the possibility of taking an empirical approach by describing our findings, as a group of researchers acting as advisors for the district of Camden in the city of London, about how different age groups navigate the city. We were looking at how children could be encouraged to ride their bicycles to school in Sommers Town, a multi-ethnic area between Euston Station and King's Cross Saint Pancras. At the end of this first part of the text, the importance of the multidimensional condition of the city will become clear, and we will see how it is, precisely, the first premise of the caring city.

A number of different authors (Hoffman et al., 2005) have claimed that there are essential and important differences between participation and engagement.[2] The first of these differences is *empowerment.*

2 The term "public engagement" is used here due to its association with a broad bibliography and rigorous, well-organized methodological descriptions.

In actions involving more public engagement, information, rewards, and decision-making capabilities are shared with participants, so they can take the initiative and make decisions to resolve future problems and improve their surroundings. Empowerment is founded on the idea of giving citizens resources and authority, opportunity and motivation, while making them co-participants in the results of their actions, contributing to their competence and satisfaction. A priori, participation doesn't have to be directed at deriving any benefit – although if it is well organized, something will always be gained from it. Public engagement, on the other hand, plans, implements, and assesses how participants can benefit.

Six years ago, Marcos Cruz, then dean of the Bartlett School of Architecture, where I teach, suggested I present a project to the Public Engagement Committee. I had already been in contact, more or less formally, with initiatives and institutions that promote citizen participation. Yet the relationship with Public Engagement Committees in the UK meant that I needed training in methodology, organization criteria and, fundamentally, evaluation criteria. According to the definition given by the National Co-ordinating Centre for Public Engagement, the term "public engagement" describes the many ways in which the benefits of higher education and research can be shared with the public. A shared condition for all their actions is that, by definition, engagement is a two-way process, involving interaction and listening, with the goal of generating mutual benefit.

The second difference is the *dual track of empowerment*. In planning its objectives, public empowerment incorporates what the benefits will be for researchers and for citizens. The public will gain knowledge, tools, and the capacity for analysis, and the researchers will be able to nourish the empirical foundations of their work, obtain evidence that is difficult to deduce only from academic literature, and increase their capacity for diagnosis and assessment.

These mutual benefits mean that the relationship between the parties is reciprocal: citizens benefit, but the researchers do as well; and both groups are aware of that fact. That is why both engagement and participation are said to generate co-creations that are bold and spontaneous, that enjoy social support and are usually exciting. (Hoffman et al., 2005). However, the merit of developing tools that enhance participants' capacities (for analysis, diagnostic and action) and that construct a well-organized and specific foundation for empirical knowledge is more characteristic of citizen engagement. What kind of participation fulfills these requirements?

We might say that the term "participation" is more general; it includes any decision-making process that involves citizens who do not have any specific academic or professional training. Citizen engagement implies that there is an acquisition of tools for assessment and action on the part of citizens and an accrual of empirical data on the part of the participating researchers. Let's look at an example to illustrate the difference: a group of, say, 100 residents are invited to make a joint decision on the color of a façade, and the protocol consists of bringing them together and asking for their votes – either all at once or spread out over time, and then dismissing them. This is a process of citizen participation, but not citizen engagement. In a second example, we bring together a group of citizens to decide on the future use of a lot in their neighborhood that has recently become public property. They are invited to a seminar on the effects of incorporating public facilities in different places internationally, and they are informed about the strategic goals of municipal planning. The deliberation process, organized in phases, helps the experts gather empirical information on the local patterns of use of the facilities (what kind of pool or library they prefer, their motivation for the choice, their opinions of the existing facilities, etc.). The second example is a case where, in addition to citizen participation, there has also been public engagement, with greater relevance and impact then if the issue was submitted to a popular vote, which all too often can end up being of little significance.[3]

These differences help to better determine the potential benefits of a paradigm of distributed power and knowledge (Champlin and Champlin, 2009), and they are essential in the academic sphere. That said, at this point, I have to admit that the fundamental difference, the one that really matters, has to do with the quality of the participation, when it has been well-planned. The kind that takes into account a large number of organizational principles and criteria.[4] It would be as important – or more so – to establish the differences between participation carried out intuitively, without mush of a methodology (and sometimes, unfortunately, without any real intention of modifying the planning) and participation following well-established criteria and properly monitored assessment methodologies that seek out an effective, honest, and relevant incorporation of a multi-dimensional criterion that originates from the population.

When I began my public engagement project, I had recently become a mother and I had spent two years travelling to London weekly with my son, where I took him to a local day care center two days a week. Naturally, during those two years I had experienced the difficulties with transportation in the city without being able to take the subway, and I decided to focus the project on something that could improve the urban experience for the parents of young children.

When I was preparing the project I discovered that many countries are trying to implement safe routes to schools to encourage children

3 In the early days of participation in the 1960s, Bachrach and Baratz distinguished between "decisions" and "non-decisions" according to the relevance and practical impact of the issues subject to participation (Bachrach and Baratz, 1963).

4 See, for example, the activities and publications the by NGO Involve, in the UK, which offer details guidelines for organizing quality participatory processes.

to walk or ride their bikes from home to school by themselves. In London, specifically, the safe routes to school aim to contribute to a larger strategy on resilience for the city. The concept of urban resilience describes the measurable ability of any urban system [...] to maintain continuity through all shocks and stresses.[5] A resilient city is one that assesses, plans and acts in order to prepare for and respond to all kinds of obstacles – whether sudden or emerging slowly over time, whether predictable or unexpected. Consequently, those cities are better prepared to protect their inhabitants and improve their lives. I wanted the project to contribute to this international and local agenda with the development of a safe route to school in the center of London, and the Public Engagement Committee at UCL introduced me to the heads of the district of Camden, who told me they were trying to do something similar in the area of Somers Town.

Somers Town is a district in central London, within the Borough of Camden. Its development was largely influenced by the presence of three train stations that connect the north of London: Euston (1838), St. Pancras (1868) and Kings Cross (1852), together with the Midland Railway goods depot (1887), next to St. Pancras, the current location of the British Library. In the recent history of Somers Town, until just 10 years ago, the two main population groups were white working-class and a Bengali contingent, although its multi-ethnic character was beginning to emerge. In the 1980s, it was an area of high crime and conflictivity, and there were multiple attempts throughout the 1990s to pacify the neighborhood and improve quality of life (Holmes, 1989). Today, the area is subject to growing gentrification, and for years local residents have remained skeptical of projects like St. Pancras International, the British Library and, more recently, the Francis Crick Institute.

5 Definition taken from UN-Habitat: https://unhabitat.org/topic/resilience-and-risk-reduction

The Biking to School project aimed to contribute to generating various safe routes to each of the eight schools in the area, involving the local community in their design. Throughout the process, citizens of all ages were invited to build their knowledge or a more profound understanding of the urban phenomenon and to become familiar with the methodologies of space syntax, with a broader definition of urban heritage, and with the management of energy in the city. Those objectives were intended to satisfy the first element required by public engagement projects – i.e., that participating citizens should acquire new tools.

Our goal, thus, was to help citizens become familiar with the series of techniques, concepts and tools which, under the name "space syntax", have been developed mainly in academic spheres to describe how spatial arrangements influence human behavior (Hillier and Hanson, 2005). That was our method for empowering participants. To guarantee that the vectors of exchange in the project also operated in the other direction, we proposed that the project could broaden the definitions of architectural heritage and urban identity used at the Bartlett School of Architecture. We wanted to make it possible for factors related to use and perception on the part of citizens and residents who engaged in activities in the surrounding area to be included among the reason for designating a building as heritage.

CHAPTER 3 WHAT DO CHILDREN SEE WHERE THE EXPERTS SEE HERITAGE?

In this chapter we will delve into the reasons for the differences in how teams of experts and citizens view perceive the city, especially in the case of young or very young people. However, I will not rely on the arrogant and condescending hypothesis that young people's knowledge of the city is somehow incomplete in comparison to the profuse knowledge of experts. On the contrary, our empirical experience confirms that the difference between experts and citizens lies in the fact that their evaluation criteria are entirely distinct: they correspond to different forms of knowledge and experience, but which likely have a similar scope and, of course, relevance. The reason the difference is asymmetrical isn't because architects and urban planners know more, but rather it is rooted in a difference in their selection of the objects of their interest. As we will see, one of the groups only sees form, where the other only sees experience. My interest is in reconnecting both spheres in order to support more holistic design criteria and expand the knowledge of experts (including those who have completed their university training) with the exhaustive and decisive empirical findings that only participation can provide.

One of the most important activities in this project were the workshops. We carried out a number of activities and manufactured a series of different supports. The first of these supports was a series of scale models representing some of the buildings in the area, which turned them into something like a mobile dollhouse. We held workshops in three different schools, which let us observe the different reactions to the activities and, in turn, improve them. The goal was for the scale models to reproduce 10 buildings that might be emblematic for different reasons. For the first workshop we built seven models, and then we asked the children and their parents what the other three should be. Among the initial models, we included the two large stations that border the area: Euston and King's Cross-Saint Pancras (over time the historical stations have come to work almost as a unit), the schools, the church of Saint Mary, the towers from the Ampthill Estate, which, at over 20 stories, are a landmark because of their height, and a small, well-known café that occupies a free-standing building, which is considered one of the protected, most visited buildings in the area.

The models had wheels and a rope, which allowed the children to move them. They were built in such a way that, on one side, the façade of the original building was reproduced to scale and the other side was left with fewer details and outfitted with less defined interior spaces. The openings that corresponded to the windows of the buildings, which in almost all cases we had made larger in scale, had been punched out, which meant that the children could insert drawings or colored paper into them, which could then be seen from the façade side.

Thanks to the work put in by Adriana Cabello, Sally Hart and myself, the models – highly detailed in their finishes – were laser cut, and we painted them by hand, adding details like squirrels, rabbits and small animals climbing up them. We also used patterned ribbon, glitter, sequins, and other materials that we knew, from experience,

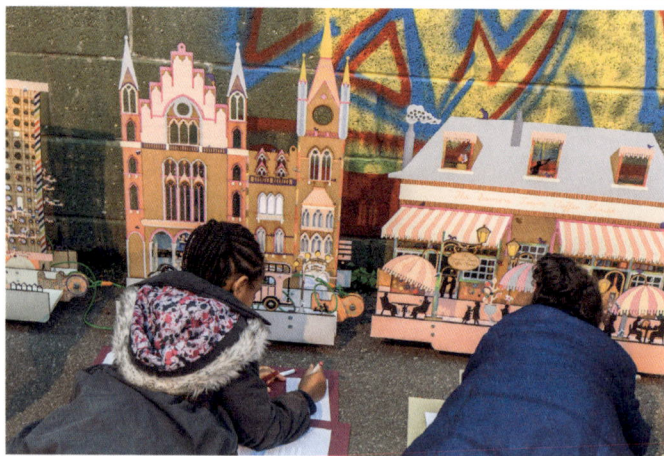

Biking to School. Workshops in Camden District. Activity with models
©Izaskun Chinchilla Architects.

would appeal to them. But in making the models we weren't just thinking about the children; we also tried to make objects that would have a certain artistic character, which would also be attractive to adults.

We used the models in the interiors where we held the workshops, but we also exhibited them on the street, before and after. The transportation of the models itself helped to drum up interest in the project. Seeing three women pulling along colorful scale models of buildings, in a line like a parade, made necessary by London's narrow sidewalks, and watching their jangling advance, bouncing around and risking breakage at every pothole, from the university to the schools or clubs where we were holding the activities, was a draw that sparked the curiosity of the community. Those decisions mean we were able to meet and talk with many people from the neighborhood and gather much more information about their opinions of their environment.

Biking to School. Workshops in Camden District. Activity with models
©Izaskun Chinchilla Architects.

The first thing we tended to do at the beginning of the workshops was asking the children to gather around the models of the buildings they knew best and to ask them and draw what was happening inside those buildings. Then, they inserted the drawings behind the windows, so they could see their drawings on the buildings' façades. As they were going about their work, Sally, Adriana, and I would go around the groups, asking them various questions. First we asked them if they recognized the building and what they thought was happening inside. Then we asked if the building had any special meaning for them that distinguished it from any others, and, if they recognized it, why it was more memorable to them than the rest.

Those conversations brought us the first surprises, the first discoveries and, I think, also the first key points. The youngest children, four- to six-year-olds, recognized the buildings based on the things they had experienced there. What they remembered about a church was that they went there on Sundays to sing with their aunt.

What they remembered about a train station was getting on the train there to take a trip. In a way, we expected these answers, but with all the attention architects pay to form, materials and appearance, we imagined that they might feel like a roof was intimidating or threatening, that they would have color preferences, or that they might think certain materials were happy or sinister.

In the children's memories, there was nothing related to the appearance, the texture, or even the color of the buildings. All the memories, which we were able to transcribe in their entirety, without exception, referred to the experiences of the children or of the people with them in the buildings: "My brother got lost in this garden once"; "My mom's happy when she comes here"; "It was boring."

When we asked the youngest children whether they remembered these buildings more than others, and why, again the answers referred to the experience. In general, children remembered the heritage buildings more if they associated them with activities that were less common: "We held a huge family reunion there"; "I had to talk into a microphone"; "That's the only time I've been on a train with the whole family".

CHAPTER 4 PARTICIPATIVE ARCHITECTURE. TECHNICAL FINDINGS AND DESIGN KEYS

After listening to the testimonies we talked about in the previous chapter, I had the feeling that, if we assume that one of the possible legitimate and fundamental purposes of architecture that aims to become collective heritage is to be remembered and used as a mnemonic landmark that helps people get their bearings in the city, architects are making some serious mistakes. In that sense, the following paragraphs begin to break down the numerous technical findings and design keys that were made possible thanks to participation. Architects and many of the agents who work in cities pay too much attention to form. This excess of attention is critical when it is in detriment to the care with which experience is planned. Below, I'm including a series of points that might help us to design and use the city in a significantly different way in that regard.

Valuing and remembering a heritage building for its form is a learned cultural behavior, whereas valuing any space based on personal experience is an innate cognitive mechanism. Only the older boys and girls, some beginning at 12 years, but mainly starting at 14, recognized the buildings with their correct names, regardless of whether they had carried out any activity there, and they were capable of offering some commentary about their formal appearance. Some even claimed that they were familiar the building because it had been pointed out to them at school or at home. This empirical finding offers new opportunities for designers who, for example, may want to promote a building being valued as a common good by different age groups or those with different cultural backgrounds: before learning to value form, children memorize their own experiences and associate them with the building.

The object of their memories aren't the features of the building, but the perceptions of the subject interacting with the architecture. Most of the authors who have looked at how architecture is perceived, many of them trained architects, have devoted their attention to its formal aspects. For example, Rasmussen, in his classic *Experiencing Architecture* (1957), pays attention to "solids, cavities, scale, proportions, rhythm". What we can learn from conversations with children is that the categories to understand what people's experience of a building are don't belong to the architecture, but to the subject perceiving them. In other words, a book about the experience of architecture should talk about ease or difficulty of orientation, about surprise, about stress or relaxation, about stimuli and sensations. It should tune into biological, cognitive and psychological aspects. Experience and memory are built with our bodies and our cognitive capacity.

When it comes to public facilities, architecture designed with an eye with to generating quality heritage, planning a good building should fundamentally consist in planning a good experience for the user. As I was rereading my notes from my conversations with children, I was reminded several times about my first visit to the Louvre with my mother. We both liked painting, and the Louvre was one of the big draws for our trip to Paris, so we set aside a full day and arrived early. When we walked into the first room my mother said to me: "I just remember my honeymoon and your dad rushing me around because we only had an hour and a half." My mother didn't remember any of the paintings or any of the spaces in the Louvre, but she vividly remembered the feeling of being rushed and the twinge of disappointment at missing out on things that she considered important. This leads me to think that making the Louvre a better building wouldn't mean adding to its already magnificent collection or extending the building with more contemporary spaces, but rather, for example, by organizing the rooms so that the most fundamental works can be viewed on a just a short tour, which is amenable, clear and summarizes, with passages into larger rooms behind each of these fundamental works for those who want to delve deeper into an author, period or movement. Perhaps then my mother's memory would have been of a pleasant space that helped her to understand, in a short time, the major aspects of the history of painting.

The beginning of a user experience doesn't coincide with entering and exiting the building. Architecture that hopes to become an articulator of the community needs to envision a scope of influence that reaches beyond the space it occupies. The most classic expression of architecture, black lines on white paper, express, in plan or section, where the rooms that make up the buildings begin and end. For a user, however, those lines in two dimensions, and their subsequent built expression, don't express the beginning and end of their perception over time. Conversations with children tell us that they may leave the house for a family celebration, get on the bus, eat a hot dog or something that is unusual for them, and go to a park – and all those spaces merge together in their memories under the single label of "the day my cousin was in London". Perhaps in their memories and in their perception, the fact of "leaving home to celebrate something with family" is more central to their experience than the physical confines of the spaces they traveled through. For architects, even when there is an emphasis on the logic of movement and *promenade*, time necessarily stops at the exterior walls of their building. And so, they need to be constantly reminded that life still goes on between one building and the next (Gehl, 2011). I believe, following these conversations, that encountering spaces for rest, protection, welcome, conversation, celebration or meeting in the areas around a building will have a significant impact on the subsequent perception of the building itself.

The experience of architecture isn't only associated with psychological stimuli, but also with group actions and socialized experiences. Many children's memories of the spaces are associated with the experiences of the group to which they felt they belonged. The main stations in the area, for example, were often associated with parents being angry or in a rush. "I remember this station. My mother was angry because we were late for the train on a weekend." The planning for a good building intended to serve the community should, therefore, take into account the socialization process of the perceptions a building awakens, reaching beyond studies that refer exclusively to the individual. Schools of architecture and urban design don't often teach about the psychology of perception, but in the few cases in which it does happen,[6] this knowledge is acquired individually by interested students, and is frequently inhibited by the limited understanding of the psychological sphere that students can achieve on their own. There is no support for formal coursework, and discussions with experts with specialized training do not usually occur. When the interest in perceptual psychology begins with students, it tends to be treated it as an individual inspiration that is intended, in large part, to differentiate the students' work, giving it a certain originality. And if the calculation is also affected by the academic curse of knowledge emerging only through practice, the individual, solitary and self-guided foray into the principles of perception tends to obstruct an analysis of its social dimension

6 Books like Merleau-Ponty's *Phenomenology of Perception* appeared in the biographies of professors such as Juan Herreros, Iñaki Ábalos or Federico Soriano, and continues to appear in the biographies of professors like Auxiliadora Gálvez or Isabella Wocek. However, its application to design is not usually included as part of a formal curriculum, but of the informal interpretation that each student engages in individually.

CHAPTER 5 THE PUBLIC AND CIVIC DIMENSIONS OF A CARING CITY AND A CARING ARCHITECTURE

The reader will note that, for the time being, no literal references to the caring city have appeared in the text. What we have presented so far can serve as the foundation, at this point, for a first working definition. Caring cities and caring architecture are those that:

- Attend to the innate capacities of human beings, although without neglecting acquired capacities, in all their diversity. A caring city and caring architecture cannot demand prior education or the acquisition of preliminary knowledge.
- The experiences that citizens of different conditions will have in the city are conceived as a fundamental part of its design.
- They understand time as continuous, in compatibility with subjective perception, incorporating what happens before and after using the building as fundamental determining factors in its design.
- Tend to and plan an area larger than what they occupy because they understand that the good experience of a building begins before entering it, as users are approaching it.
- They study experience not only in its individual dimensions, but also as a social construct, using well-planned and monitored

SOMERS TOWN.
CYCLE TO SCHOOL
project.

EMPOWERING THE 2000-2010 GENERATION –
URBAN AND DOMESTIC LEGACY IN LONDON BOROUGHS.

AT BRILL PLACE

about the project.

The project uses analysis and data gathering to build up robust research evidence in developing an understanding of patterns of human activity and use, accessibility, and cultural identity. Observations of the area throughout the project are visualised through mappings using space syntax analysis and the observation data. The resulting data is used in the project but will be also available in the project's website and blog, creating a re-source of research and future collaborations with the council, public engagement projects within UCL and the wider academic community. The signals will perform a number of functions including:

- Helping children find the most suitable route.
- Encouraging the community to discover Somers Towns' unique and often unrecognized heritage features.
- Discovering the spatial and multicultural richness of Somers Town.

public engagement.

The project aims to explore Somers Town in its current form, discovering unrecognized heritage such as virtual representation in cinema, internet or literature, multicultural appropriations and historic events. But more importantly, it reflects on what the urban and domestic legacy of today´s children could be, and will design and fabricate components that encourage them to believe that they can influence their city. they own their neighbourhood.

space syntax methodology.

Space syntax theory and methodologies are used to analyse the spatial accessibility of the street network in Somers Town, collect empirical data of human activity, study the relationship between spatial accessibility, activity and movement, and visualize results and evidence. The analysis led to guidelines and strategies for way-finding and visualisation for the community of the day-to-day functioning of their neighbourhood. The proposed project seeks to develop a longitudinal analysis, building the base for future work, transferring knowledge from this research to the Council and local community and engage sustainable communities in this process.

about us.

The Bartlett School of Architecture, University College London (UCL) and Camden Council are working together on a Cycle to School Project to help find the answers to these questions and to make your trip to and from school more fun, safe, healthy and educational.

For more information about the project visit CYCLING TO SCHOOL BLOG.
https://blogs.ucl.ac.uk/cycling-to-school

Contact us:
Izaskun Chinchilla : i.moreno@ucl.ac.uk
Sally Hart: sally.hart@ucl.ac.uk
Adriana Cabello: a.plasencia@ucl.ac.uk

Somers Town Sports Day workshop.

COME AND JOIN US FOR AN AFTERNOON OF GAMES ABOUT YOU AND YOUR NEIGHBOURHOOD!

WEDNESDAY 26TH OF AUGUST.
from 12.00pm -5pm

How well do you know the streets around where you live and go to school?

How do you get around?

How could your trip to school be made better?

What would make you want to ride a bike more?

Workshop
Parents for Sport at Ampthill Square

Workshop
Plot 10 Community Play Project

Workshop
Parents for Sport at Ampthill Square

Biking to School. Workshops in Camden District. Activity with models
©Izaskun Chinchilla Architects.

participatory methods to inform the design, in order to better grasp this social dimension of experience.

I would like to round out this initial definition of caring architecture and the caring city – which, as readers can imagine, will have a multidimensional pronouncement – incorporating some more political aspects concerning its public and civic dimensions. In order to delve into these other dimensions we will turn our attention back to workshops and empirical work. As we explained earlier, we held four workshops. The first of them, dating from November 2014, was held at PLOT 10, an after-school club for children. The participants were 20 boys and girls between the ages of 7 and 11 and two 5-year-olds. Parents did not attend the workshop, but we had the opportunity to speak with them at pick-up. The second workshop, in January 2015, was held at the Parents for Sport association, another after-school club, run by Águeda Hurtado in the area of Ampthill Towers, with deep ties to the community, involved the participation of five mothers and 23 children between the ages of 4 and 14. The third workshop, coinciding with Sports Day at Brill Place Park, was supposed to take place outdoors at the end of August, but it rained heavily and we were only able to include six boys and girls between 8 and 11 years old, all of whom cycled often. The fourth workshop, in September 2015, coincided with Community Day and the participants took part as a family, in a park. More than 30 families were involved, with children and parents of a variety of ages.

The first activity, detailed in the previous chapter, was based on exploring the scale models that looked like dollhouses. Subsequently, we asked the girls to move the models of the heritage buildings and place them on a large map of Somers Town that we laid out on the ground. The map was completed as we carried out further workshops. In the last two sessions we set up the map before the workshop started, using wooden pieces to represent intersections and strips running between them to symbolize the streets. Both on the four arms of the intersection pieces and on the strips that stood in for the streets, we had engraved the street names using laser technology. Thus, the map offered a schematic representation of the city in two-dimensions, structured through intersections and streets labelled with their corresponding names. The size of the map and its position on the ground meant that the children could walk across it and even ride their bicycles over it, which they loved. Before situating the models of the heritage buildings, we asked the children to reproduce their routes from home to school by walking across the map. Most of the children who could locate their house and school on the map and retrace their route were 10 years old or older, although there were some exceptions with children who we able interpret the map at 8 years old.

Participants over the age of 10 were usually the first to find the locations of major landmarks like Euston Station or King Cross. But, as more models were placed on the map, younger children were

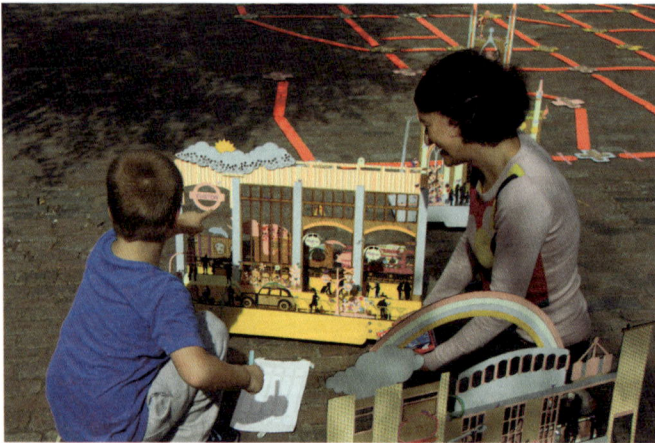

Biking to School. Workshops in Camden District. Activity with models
©Izaskun Chinchilla Architects.

able to locate their schools or churches using inferences like "it's on the street behind the station," because the street names were often not meaningful to them. The more three-dimensional elements the map contained, the easier it was for the younger children to deduce the correct location of another element. Once all the models were in place, beginning at 6 or 7 years old the children were able to reproduce, approximately, their routes from home to school. This experience gave us an enormous amount of data on how children perceive the city and its representations, which we will discuss further in the following chapters.

Biking to School. Workshops in Camden District. Activity with models
©Izaskun Chinchilla Architects.

CHAPTER 6 BOOKS THAT CHILDREN HAVE MADE US RE-READ

The empirical observations from our workshops should lead us to reflect on the public role of buildings in the city. It's clear that, in the design, transformation and rehabilitation of buildings, the fundamental objectives include the satisfaction of the needs of their inhabitants, owners and tenants. Aside from that function, however, because buildings exist within an urban environment, they play social roles that affect not only their tenants, owners or inhabitants in the "first-degree". Numerous authors have explored the varied aspects of the public dimension of buildings. From 1960 to 1980, a wide range of literature was published dedicated to reviewing the dimensions, aspects, capacities, and civic obligations of architecture that modern functionalism had left behind over the previous three decades. In our conversations with the children, we were able to confirm the enduring relevance of some of those authors' claims.

Our workshops called to mind three of those descriptions of the public dimension of architecture. In 1960, Kevin Lynch defended the need for city residents to construct a template or a coherent mental image of the city to be able to navigate through it: "In the process of way-finding, the strategic link is the environmental image, the generalized mental picture of the exterior physical world that is held by the individual. This image is the product both of immediate sensation and of the memory of past experience, and it is used to interpret information and to guide action." In the construction of this mental image, Lynch attributes to buildings – especially unique, heritage buildings – the condition of landmarks, structural points in the urban pattern and in the definition of routes through the city. Indeed, the children found it much easier to navigate through the city when the building models were situated on the map. Frequently, the children used them as articulating elements in the descriptions of their routes: ("First we go down a wide street until we get to the church, and then we take the narrow street until we get to the school").

Once the models were situated on the map, we used them to ask the children, as we explained earlier, to show us their routes from school to home. During this exercise, the segments that represented the streets appeared green. When they had finished with their explanations, we showed them that the segments that represented the streets could be flipped over to turn them red. We asked them to reflect on whether there were any points along the route that they found unpleasant, that made them feel fear, anxiety or a sense of danger. We detected two fundamental types of spaces that the children considered unpleasant: spaces with the most traffic; and spaces adjacent to blind façades, buildings without windows, openings onto the street, or elements that connect interior and exterior.

This is evidence that Jane Jacobs explicitly highlights, granting buildings the almost civic obligation of being "eyes upon the street": "The buildings on a street equipped to handle strangers and to insure the safety of both residents and strangers, must be oriented to the street. They cannot turn their backs or blank sides on it and leave it blind." It is significant that Jane Jacobs was a woman and a mother. Part of the very important book that she offered to the international community in 1961 contains the kind of empirical knowledge that also emerged in the workshops we organized. The academic community in architecture and urban planning took three decades to incorporate many of the proposals that she presented and defended early on. This happened, in part, because her source of knowledge – her experience as a user of the city – was denied legitimacy, along with her capabilities, acquired without the auspices of a university degree, which let her express herself with such unique liveliness: her analytical ability, her penchant for reading, and the journalistic skills she had acquired while working, among other assignments, as editor of *Architectural Forum*. Lewis Mumford bitterly criticized *The Death and Life of Great American Cities* in the *New Yorker* with the headline "Mother Jacobs' Home Remedies".[7] We will reflect on this issue again later.

Norberg-Schulz and Charles Jencks perhaps most famously defended the fundamental role of architecture in the construction of the identity of a community or region, arguing that when buildings do not contribute to the construction of that identity, they leave citizens "without a world of their own", bereft of the sense of belonging to the community and lacking any desire to participate. In the stories that the children told about their routes to school, this notion is confirmed, with a special intensity when it came to the buildings that housed schools. The children developed a very strong attachment to their schools, felt pride in belonging, used its symbols and invariably believed that the architecture of their own school was more beautiful than others and, moreover, it represented much more important values, which were more characteristic of the neighborhood. That same affiliation was present for places they associated an intense experience, and around which a sense of community had been constructed. For example, the children living in Ampthill Towers

7 "Mother Jacobs' Home Remedy for Urban Cancer" http://www.notablebiogra- phies. com/supp/Supplement-Fl-Ka/Jacobs-Jane.html#ixzz4tBumacfF

showed enormous pride in living in the towers and belonging to their community.

The juxtaposition of conversations with children and academic readings allows, at least, for defining three axes on which the public, urban and civic role of buildings centers. On the one hand, they contribute to structuring perception: they allow citizens to break down a complex itinerary into smaller sections, using their position as a point of reference, making them fundamental components in the mental image we develop of the city. The buildings also support coexistence in the community because the configuration of their entrances, exits, openings, exterior spaces, open-air or covered areas qualifies the surrounding space. Additionally, the architecture can become a symbol that builds an identity for the community, helping to bring its members together and represent them.

How do buildings combine these three public roles? Their form, their openings, and the quantity and the quality of their details comprise and support these three fundamental social functions. But their effectiveness depends, in the light of interviews, conversations and readings, on specific circumstances.

The relational reading of the building: form and singularity as part of the pattern. Here it is worth recalling that when we asked young children about their memories of a building, about whether they liked it or why, their answers hardly ever depended on factors related to the buildings' form. In other words, even when the conversations and questions took place in the presence of the individual models of the buildings, curiously, the formal aspects were largely insignificant in how memorable a building was. The formal aspects began to gain importance once the conversations and questions were taken onto the map, as they tried to piece together the details of their routes and how they use the buildings in constructing their mental image.

Working on a flat surface that the children could walk over or ride their bikes over, we detected that buildings with a certain heritage quality and a more pronounced formal singularity were more useful in the organization of their routes. The children often said things like "I leave the house and walk down the wide street until I get to the corner where I fell that time," as opposed to "I leave the house and walk down the wide street until I get to the church." In other words, we found that when the children talked about individual buildings, specific events and anecdotes – their personal recollections – take on an extraordinary importance in the construction of their memory of the building; however, when it comes to articulating their routes, they tend to internalize more stable references, which do not change over time.

Our conversations with the children lead us to conjecture that the perception of the form of buildings in the city is internalized according to a structure that is based on both spatial and temporal patterns. When it comes to constructing a memory of a building, the episode "I fed a bird that was sitting on the fence there" is valuable and reliable; but when I need to remember the path to school, I rely on observations that have been repeated more often, like "I turn in front of the church." Perception in the form of patterns can also be applied in spatial terms. Young citizens don't focus on the form of an element; instead, they internalize a pattern and perceive that a particular building represents an irregularity in that pattern. As a result, when they are asked about the building, they can't point out much about it specifically because, in reality, what they are perceiving is the regularity or irregularity it represents within a larger pattern.

When the building is seen in isolation, little remains of that accumulated information. The children didn't say "I turn when I come to a building with a roof that's different from the others" or "I turn when I come to a building that isn't directly between two others like the rest," however, in reality, those unique elements were more useful to them when it came to structuring their routes. Formal singularity contributes to this differentiating and articulating function: taller buildings or free-standing buildings that aren't between party walls and stand out from the surrounding fabric, are, of course, more likely to be used as landmarks. The appreciation of this formal distinction operates on an unconscious plane; it is relevant in terms of orientation but it is not mentioned or made explicit. And, of course, it is not perceived as a value in itself, but is internalized as an element that aids in interpreting the pattern. These observations are supported by the literature that upholds patterns, and their mental characterizations, as playing a key role in how we understand our surroundings: "The pattern, and it alone, brings into being, and causes to pass away, and confers purpose, that is to say, value and meaning, on all there is. To understand is to perceive patterns. [...] To make intelligible is to reveal the basic pattern" (Berlin, 2000).

The permeability of the building from public space. Buildings determine the quality and character of public space. In defining the quality of the topological relationship between private and public space, the discipline of space syntax looks at characteristics such as topological depth, the degree of intervisibility between entrances and windows, the degree of constitution, the layout of the streets and their function, the density of entrances connected to the exterior, the intervisibility from windows in parking areas and the degree of territoriality (Nes, 2008).

Likewise, constituted street segments are those that have numerous entrances and exits from the adjoining buildings and a large number of windows. In contrast, unconstituted street segments run in front of blank façades. The more entrances are connected to a street, the greater the probability that someone will exit a private space into a public one. The workshops confirmed that, from a very early age, children tend to see unconstituted street segments as inhospitable spaces.

However, a high density of entrances connected to a street does not always imply high intervisibility. The areas the children deemed pleasant on their routes to school included many street segments lined with windows and, almost invariably, sections where the houses have individual entrances, and, above all, where the windows provide views of the interiors of the houses. In space syntax, the term "topological depth" is used to define this condition, which young citizens cited as pleasant in our conversations, in which public space participates in interior life.

In their designs, architects tend to emphasize the sense of privacy within the context of modern life. The explanation can often be found in the individualization process of human beings that has taken place in Western society over the last 60 years. When we live together with other people, a large degree of privacy seems to be necessary. However, when the city offers increased anonymity, we may begin to wonder whether it is necessary to hide away a house's door or windows from public streets (Nes, 2008).

The spatial relationships between buildings and streets play a crucial role in the socioeconomic life of human beings. The concept of recovering the human scale is often used in urban policy making. It refers to the theoretical properties of space. But a better understanding of urban life can be gained through a topological approach on the urban micro-scale. Specifically, urban renewal projects, modern-style residential areas, and large-scale development projects tend to reduce the permeability and visibility between buildings and streets. This has negative effects both on life on the street and on safety, as well as on the perception of environmental quality and the construction of a feeling of connection and belonging.

A distinctive character and quality. Form is not the only factor that leads city residents to use certain buildings more than others to articulate their routes. Many of the buildings that are perceived as points of reference within the pattern display a more elaborate architecture, with more details and a more careful construction. Children tend to take as their points of reference buildings that have more elements to focus on. In other words, buildings in which the design and construction of windows, fences, doors, accessory elements, façade materials, articulations, etc., seem to have been thought out, premeditated, and attended to in response to an intention. In general, the children tended to prefer street segments that coincided with older architecture, pre-modern buildings, or new constructions with a certain richness in detail. From an anthropological point of view, the reading of the texts by Lévi-Strauss and the beautiful reflections of what he calls the *house society* show us that the kind of architecture that has the capacity to unite communities around it tends to be very elaborate in terms of details and in the incorporation of elements that may, at first glance, be considered decorative. Although with the extensive regulations and legislative frameworks we have developed, our societies are far removed from the ones described by Lévi-Strauss, where houses set the guidelines for the community in the absence of an explicit regulatory codification. The principle of elaborate architecture makes it possible to combine identity and a certain sense of pride for the community, and it can be applied to any human environment.

This is a point that should be cause for reflection among architects, who will be taught to love abstraction at architecture school, as Edward Ford aptly reminds us: "The means to abstraction in architecture and in detailing is elimination." (Ford, 2009). By eliminating details, those small elements that characterize a more elaborate architecture, designed and built more slowly, we are also eliminating the possibility for those buildings to qualify, articulate and structure citizens' perceptions.

Details are, in turn, an unquestionable source of identity construction both for the community on a small scale and for the city on a larger scale. The quality and profusion of these details are what, at least for ordinary citizens, distinguishes architecture that is worth preserving from the kind that can be renovated without too many qualms.

These three aspects should be food for thought for architects. User experience contradicts the doctrine that is taught about form, intimacy and abstraction in architecture schools. Architects should understand that form isn't a value in itself, but rather the key for interpreting, distinguishing, differentiating and consolidating patterns. There needs to be a serious and in-depth review of the criteria of intimacy and interrelation and of how architectural design, along with urban planning, prevent urban life from occurring with the spontaneity it had in traditional dense and compact cities. Finally, the recent preference for abstract architecture without detailing, and the criminalization of ornament,[8] leave citizens without the possibility of identifying, precisely, with the distinguishing factor that helped them recognize that a building had value for the community.

Let's review these new dimensions that we have attributed to caring architecture and the caring city – specifically, those aspects that have a bearing on their public status.

8 It is truly surprising to me that Adolf Loos's text, "Ornament and Crime", is still considered a classic of architectural thought at architecture schools and that it is still upheld today and practically undisputed.

Caring architecture and the caring city:

- Contribute consciously and intentionally to constructing patterns and exceptions that support navigation and orientation in the city.

- Balance public and private interests in the city, actively taking into account not only the needs of first-degree users (owners, tenants or direct users), but also those of all citizens.

- Are permeable, permitting a connection between private and public activities.

- Show enough quality, detail and uniqueness to be considered an admirable, shared achievement by the community that uses them and to contribute to the construction of identity.

CHAPTER 7 WHAT DO WE LOSE WHEN THE CITY AND ARCHITECTURE AREN'T MADE TO BE CARING?

After our first two workshops we began to realize that the discoveries we made about our cities as a result of children's participation would contain something unsettling. We began to see that the cities we live in were wasting the potential of the youngest members of their population, who, systematically and at every age, had capabilities that surpassed what was allowed or recommended for them in their current uses of the city. This led us to design specific activities to detect the gaps between what children are capable of and what they actually do in cities.

One of the last activities we carried out during our workshops was to ask the children, using the map that we had built on the ground and in which we had situated the models of the heritage buildings, to navigate from their school to places they were familiar with, but which were not represented on the map. We asked them to go to restaurants or friends' houses they had mentioned in previous conversations. At first we didn't make any suggestions; then if they couldn't get their bearings, we gave them references using street names. If that wasn't sufficient, we used landmarks. If the verbal instructions were unsuccessful, we showed them a map of the area and indicated the route. For the littlest ones, we did an axonometric drawing, which they could take with them and which served as a guide, incorporating lots of three-dimensional elements.

This final activity, together with the previous experiences, helped us to reach some conclusions about the capabilities of children of different ages when it comes to autonomous orientation. We were also able to look at how well they could understand directions and how the format of those directions (verbal, graphic, two-dimensional or volumetric) empowers children of different ages. Personally, I have had the great fortune of corroborating our conclusions by walking with my son, and with friends and their children of different ages.

These are the conclusions we drew:

4-year-olds:

- They are able to associate buildings with personal experiences and stories related to their lives.
- They tend to appreciate and value a building based on the experiences they have had ("They visited with their family", "They play there", "It's their school", "They have gone there to sing with their aunt").
- Depending on the activity carried out in the buildings, they are associated with feelings: fear, calm, happiness.
- They are capable of recalling routes that they have memorized because they have repeated them many times, although it is possible, even easy, for them to become disoriented.
- When it comes to mnemonic orientation, they do not distinguish between temporary memories and memories that persist in a place. For example, their memory of a particular a corner may be that there was a bird perched there.
- They have a sense of orientation based on memory. If they want to go to the park and they are given the choice of taking a different street than usual, they tend to insist on going the usual way.

- They are able to relate a building to its three-dimensional representation.
- They are capable of associating a building with some of its planimetric representations, such as the elevation, and even sometimes, although in very few cases, with the floor plan.

5/6-year-olds:

- They are able to explain why they like or dislike a building. The criteria still draw on personal experience and private anecdotes much more than on the building itself.
- They are capable of recalling routes that they have memorized because they have repeated them a few times, and it is less likely they will become disoriented.
- They begin to memorize points of references in places: they internalize patterns and distinguish not only landmarks but also areas. They begin to differentiate between the things that persist in the city and the things that change and orient themselves more by what remains.
- Their sense of orientation is improved, and they are better able to identify directions, even on the streets that they or their families do not typically use.
- They are capable of relating a building with its three-dimensional representation and orienting it, identifying the back, the entrance, and which street it faces.
- They are able to associate the building with some of its planimetric representations, such as the elevation and, on many occasions, the floor plan. They begin to recognize entrances and spaces on a floor plan.
- They are able to name some landmarks if they have been shown them by their parents or have become familiar with them at school.

8-year-olds:

- They are able to name major neighborhood landmarks when they see them in a picture or in a model. Some of the names are not the official ones, but rather related to their personal experience, but, in general, the nomenclature they use for many landmarks is correct.
- They exclusively use elements that persist in orienting themselves, differentiating temporary aspects as "unreliable".
- They are capable of navigating on the three-dimensional map, associating the routes represented in an axonometric view with the routes they take in the real city. It is not so easy for them to do the same on a two-dimensional map, although some are very good at it.
- They are usually unable to describe their route from memory if it is long, but they can follow clues on the map.

9-year-olds:

- They are able to read a map.
- They are normally unable to map out their route on a two-dimensional map, but they can reproduce it on the three-dimensional map.
- They understand the concept of urban points of reference and are able to orient themselves using the models situated within the three-dimensional map.

10/11-year-olds:

- They are able to identify places in the city that they use as points of reference but which are not included in the list of monuments prepared by the workshop's organizers.

13-year-olds:

- They begin to use street names.

14/15-year-olds:

- This is usually the age when they are allowed to move around on their own, sometimes to school, almost always only for short trips in the neighborhood where they live.
- They are generally able to describe their routes from memory, interpret maps and use street names.

This is, of course, a very generic description of abilities by age, for which there are many exceptions. I am also aware that the number of participants and the methodology used in their selection have important shortcomings, which prevents these observations from being used universally. But these descriptions are not intended to establish a scholastic classification of abilities by age; but rather, and fundamentally, they are meant to highlight something that we consider very relevant: that children begin doing things in cities much later than what their abilities would allow, and that there are supports and formats (models, three-dimensional representations) that advance their capacity for action in the city.

One of the major conclusions from our workshops is, for example, that children have the ability to make very simple trips around the city from the age of 4, and yet they are not usually allowed to do so until they are 14. The optimal thing for the cognitive development of children would be for them to begin realizing short independent routes at the age of 4 years. In traditional villages, this was the age when children first began to carry out errands on their own: buying bread or fetching milk at a store that was close by and familiar to them. In our cities, many of the things that children can do from the time they are four years old do not begin, de facto, until they are 14. The conversations with parents were especially revealing for analyzing the reasons for this delay. Fundamentally, they alleged the risks of road safety and the children's' physical and emotional integrity (it goes without saying, but parents are afraid their children will be physically or psychologically harmed). The question that should be asked in the wake of these partial conclusions is: Is it worth delaying the cognitive development of the entire population of a city so that a small percentage of its inhabitants can drive to work? Who, when, and with what legitimacy, decided that the rights of working-age men come before those of many of the other groups that coexist in, inhabit, sustain, populate, and enliven the city? How can cities and their architecture contribute to the physical and psychological integrity of all their inhabitants?

The next part of this book will be devoted to this discussion. For now, these last reflections should serve to contribute to this multidimensional definition of caring architecture and the caring city by looking at the definition of what might be called *indifferent architecture and urbanism*. Its characteristics include:

- Failing to consider the capacities, desires and needs of different population groups in its configuration, placing priority in a generalized and abusive way on satisfying the objectives of particular social groups without accounting for their actual representativeness, in either numerical or qualitative terms.

- Failing to provide support, through public information, signage or through the urban configuration, for understanding the different possibilities of use and undermining citizen empowerment by way of a medium that is difficult to read and interpret.

Part Two

Nest: Shaping the Caring City

INTRODUCTION SEVEN OBJECTS AND IDEAS FOR TRANSFORMING THE CITY

In the wake of decades of industrialization, our cities, in their physical and legislative dimensions, are places geared towards productivity. In cities, it is possible – in material terms and relatively easily in the course of daily life – to deliver merchandise, put up advertising announcing a commercial activity, or drive to work. There are rules that regulate these activities, which permit and even promote their performance, and which tell us how, when and where we must carry them out. These rules aim to strike a balance between individual rights and collective interests.

Our cities are a more hostile environment for activities that are not associated with production: trying to sleep in, using a service, drinking clean water free of charge, breathing unpolluted air, having fun without consuming, or walking without getting wet on a rainy day, are all feats in today's city. The regulatory interest in these "non-productive" practices has been marginal. When there are regulations that have a bearing on these activities, their intent is generally prohibition or limitation.

Prioritizing productive activities in the city has meant that citizens have been defined as individuals who contribute to productivity. They are plumbers, delivery people, merchants or employees. Biological (age, gender, race, health) and subjective characteristics (personality, tastes, affective networks) are not accounted for in the formation, regulation, and governance of the city. This negation does not occur only in practical terms: the problem is not limited to the fact that the city is difficult to use for people whose vision is impaired or who do not handle stress well. The negation of the biological and subjective dimensions of city residents has been socialized and normalized to the point of becoming a cultural principle – and one that is fundamentally tied to politics.

Productive activities are prioritized in the legislation of the city, and, as a result, more rights are granted to those who, historically, have dominated those activities. The regulations that are enforced in the city aim to avoid urban abuses; for example, there are prohibitions on the construction, sale, or rental of housing that is unsanitary or that is overcrowded so someone can earn a lot of money quickly. They aim to ensure that the goods required for the operations of pharmacies or supermarkets arrive in a timely manner at their destination and that daily commutes are reasonably efficient so that people can get to work on time. Who has traditionally carried out these activities (investment, logistics and employment), which are the focus political attention? Non-immigrant men of working age, with a certain amount of purchasing power and, more often than not, without any atypical physical or cognitive conditions. By basing our regulations on the observation of a particular type of activity, we are granting an implicit political role to the actors who traditionally carry out those tasks. The needs of other actors are not observed with the same attention: cities don't offer safe spaces for people who might be lost, places for taking a nap, or public toilets. Why is that? Because hidden behind the apparent and official idea that the city is regulated to protect a universal citizen, in reality, the fact is that the city has been regulated to protect the actors who carry out productive activities: people who don't get lost, who don't need a rest halfway to their destination, and who can pay for a drink at a café if they need to use the bathroom. In institutional decision-making processes – which can include the design of the city – the universal representation of a city dweller has been affected by this bias, and it coincides with the main actor in productive activities.

Cities have gradually turned any physical and cognitive characteristics that diverge from the profile of the typical productive actor into features of vulnerability. Being four years old is not, in principle, a shortcoming, but the city turns that into a vulnerability because four-year-olds may be run over by cars, they make get lost easily, or someone could kidnap them or convince them to do things they shouldn't. The mechanism at work is simple: it generates a context in which the needs of one group are made a priority and, because the context ignores the satisfaction of the needs of the rest, those other groups acquire traits of vulnerability, which are derived from the characteristics of the context. It is important to recall and insist that citizens cannot be defective: not having a home, not speaking a language, being a child or an elderly person, not hearing well, or not being able to walk are not deficiencies per se. It is the context that turns citizens' characteristics into vulnerabilities. With a change of setting – for example, on a beach – a four-year-old girl may be better adapted to the environment than a 45-year-old bank manager. Cities and their forms make citizens weak or strong unequally.

This finding places a great responsibility in the hands of the agents who design the city: our decisions and our management distribute opportunities unequally among citizens. However, and this is the focus of the second part of this book, they can also open up a vast field of opportunities. The design of the human habitat can empower all kinds of users, and a thoughtful, well-advised and properly assessed exercise of urban governance can contribute to making sure everyone's rights are respected. This is a complex challenge, almost infinite even, for several reasons. The first is that there an unlimited number of potential distinctive traits among citizens. The second is that the resources available at any given time are, always and by definition, limited. The second part of this book offers the illustration of a possible start down that path, which can never be deemed as complete. It lays out a beginning based on two fundamental premises: the structural value of diversity, and the austerity of resources. The following pages will propose actions for transforming the city in which the biological, physical and cognitive differences between citizens are values to be promoted and preserved through design, and which, moreover, can be financed by small budgets. These actions could be just the beginning of a profound transformation of our cities, of a conversion whose implementation should be much more ambitious.

To set out on the path toward transforming our cities into caring cities, this part will propose transforming seven common objects in our urban environments. It may seem surprising that, in aspiring to a major social and political transformation, this text begins with an invitation to look at objects – and objects, what's more, that have an apparently limited importance and scope. This opening shares its perspective with the sociology of technology and innovation, including authors like Bruno Latour, who have argued that material objects, perhaps even more than ideologies, condition our modes of action, our agendas, what we consider possible, what we consider legal or ethical. Objects, de facto, actively mediate between our intentions and our actions. The transformation of small urban elements can, therefore, lead to a shift in major citizen agendas, perhaps more effectively than ideological affirmations.

The titles of each of the following seven sections will include the object to be transformed, and a proposal for its modification. These proposals are not exemplary or intended to solve all urban problems; they are possible proposals meant to help us recombine the rights that the city grants to its users based on hierarchies that are different from the current ones.

Instructive, Fenced In, and Segregated Playground

Different critics have pointed out that children's play and its integration into daily life is one of the great casualties of the prioritization of productive tasks in the development of the city (Tonucci, 2015; Voce, 2015). The harm is two-fold. On the one hand, as uses considered non-priority, they are not given the ideal locations or conditions. Instead, they are allocated those sites that are not useful for the functions considered of central importance to the city. On the other hand, there is an application of a translation of functionalist and productive thinking, in which educational aspects take precedence, and control and safety are more important than enjoyment or overall development. This second type of harm is almost more serious because it shows, in reality, that, when it comes to designing playgrounds, the interests of productive citizens once again prevail: they shouldn't be too fun, they should steer clear of fully developing children's capabilities, and, above all, they should avoid taking up the experts' time and attention. The priority of production has an enormous functional, cultural, philosophical and political effect.

The group Solasgune[9] defines the problems with current urban playgrounds by highlighting three aspects:

- They are *instructive* play areas – that is, we tell the children how they should be playing (climb up here, slide down there, move these pieces, fit these shapes together, swing here) on each of the elements.
- They are *fenced in* and located in specific areas of the city. In that sense, they construct a discontinuous vision of play. Their design invites children to play when they enter and to stop playing when they leave.
- Users are *segregated* by age.

Those of us who have spent long hours in children's playgrounds know that the most fun comes from the unexpected uses of the spaces, which, otherwise, are very often no longer exciting on the second or third visit. Children have fun climbing onto the top of a playhouse that was designed for pretending to cook inside it, watching how balls bounce off it or how sand forms waterfalls as it falls off the roof. Those activities may be interesting three or four times if they aren't shared with someone else, but they can lead to hours, or days, of exciting, even frenetic, activity when shared with a friend. Although today's playgrounds offer a basic type of interaction that has a certain value, they lack two very important elements that children look for when it comes to a richer and more significant interaction: personalized and imaginative risk management; and the development of tools for socialization. Authors like Robin Moore (1978) have compared the types of interaction in these playgrounds (instructive, fenced in, and segregated) with the activities that children carry out in a forest or a natural space, highlighting the

9 Solasgune is a multidisciplinary team of people who, since 1996, have been working in the community and in learning environments to promote relationships of trust and individual and collective creativity.

enormous advantages of the latter, among other things because of the two factors mentioned above: risk management and sociability.

Additionally, authors like Moore highlight the advantages of interactions in a natural environment because they provide a more complete sensory experience and a greater cognitive challenge, calling on abilities like orientation, inference (by observing rabbits, I learn that it is easier to find them where there are holes in the ground), and deduction (if I know moss grows on the north side of trees, I can orient myself by looking at tree trunks). Moore also highlights the ability of natural environments to promote emotional connections: Is there anyone who doesn't feel a special attachment to the landscapes they were introduced to as a child (Moore, 1989)?

It seems that interactions in the nature have served as a point of reference for those who defend free and open play. Not surprisingly, as a child, Marjory Gill – the future Lady Allen of Hurtwood who would become the godmother of free play – lived on a farm with her extended family, surrounded by affection and a sense of security, and plenty of opportunities for fun. This experience led her to devote her life to defending the creation of play areas where activities were not predefined. For her, playgrounds should keep curiosity alive and therefore must incorporate a dose of unpredictability. Plus, free play helps you learn things about your own rhythms.

Francesco Tonucci also makes an interesting point: the most dangerous places for children today are their homes and their parents' cars. Those places are, in fact, where most accidents occur.

Today's fenced playgrounds also contain an implicit definition of the conditions of care: adults look after children. The action occurs unilaterally, and the type of care is associated with surveillance. The fences around playgrounds imply that adults will make sure their children do not leave the safe area. Once inside, children are told what to do and where to do it, and they are prevented from coming into contact with people who have more developed abilities. We have a problem: our administrations don't fully understand the love between parents and their children, what its rules are; moreover, our administrations don't consider it one of their obligations to understand the nature of love.

Amy Mullin, an interesting Canadian philosopher who pays special attention to care-related activities, highlights the lack of official reflection, in general, on love and affection – and, in particular, on love that is not romantic or does not involve a heterosexual couple. Mullin (2007) says that we tend to think of children as passive agents in receiving care. This view ignores the finding, obtained by psychologists through empirical observation, that, before two years of age, children are capable of adapting their preferences and the satisfaction of their own desires to ensure greater happiness for the people with whom they have a significant bond (Mullin, 2006). Likewise, the current functional view of care ignores the pleasure and benefits that adults obtain in their dealings with children. Children also take care of adults in a very active way: they give them affection, worry about them, and try to have a good time with them (fun times that are shared are much more interesting). Amy Mullin grants a certain symmetry or horizontal quality to care relationships: when they are properly focused and understood, everyone involved in care pursues the well-being of the others, even at the cost of their own personal preferences. The relationships implicit in a typical urban playground are profoundly asymmetrical and vertical. They are asymmetrical because children cannot provide adults with the same good things they are experiencing. They can't challenge their mother to a race, for example, if they know that she likes to run. The relationships are vertical because adults have a practical monopoly over responsibility. By eliminating risk and segregating by age, it exempts children from taking responsibility for their own safety and that of others and for the satisfaction of adult needs.

Pixels of Nature in the City

Lady Allen of Hurtwood (1971) reminded us that children play wherever they go. Planning the city with the aim of encouraging play implies thinking about how children can play in all the spaces where they inhabit (leisure spaces, stairways, walls, balconies, squares). When children play, they introduce content into the context: their surroundings take on a symbolic value. The meaning associated with the place depends on the players' actions. Playgrounds should be sequences of open stimuli that accompany families in their movements, and to which children give meaning, either on their own or in a horizontal interaction with one another and with adults.

Fortunately, pigeons, puddles, stairs, or ramps are stimuli that appear spontaneously in the city and that can contribute to the construction of these sequences. But we should ask ourselves where these spontaneous stimuli are least likely to appear or – more importantly – what effects and benefits might come from the existence of these stimuli in places where they are not usually found.

As in other sections of the second part of this book, this text offers a specific proposal: we believe that play in the city can benefit enormously from the inclusion of small natural spaces that are well distributed across the city. This would make it possible for children to engage in a more continuous playful activity, sustained by the stimuli they would come across with a certain frequency. Adults could also participate in the play, exercise, or take advantage of a stop to make a call. It would be ideal to insert these pixels of nature into places where adults, or "units of cohabitation and care", have responsibilities to fulfill. Let's look at some examples together: we might set up 12 m² of productive garden space in front of a town hall; an equivalent space of beach sand in the inner courtyard of a post office; and a small square with a splash pad in the garden outside the Tax Authority or the Social Security administration. Now let's think about what might happen: while a father is in the town hall, a grandfather and a granddaughter can smell the tomatoes; a mother and son can spend 15 minutes barefoot in the sand after picking up a certified letter; an entrepreneur can resolve her doubts about a VAT payment while her two children wade in a fountain in a protected glass area that she can keep an eye on.

The ideas for the current locations of playgrounds in the city only take into account the possibility that children will be instructed. It is important to remember that there are roughly 175 school days in a year in most Spanish autonomous communities, the minimum established by the Spanish laws on education. Let's do some math: that leaves our children with about 190 school-free days each year, 104 of which coincide with weekends. That leaves 86 weekdays a year when our children are not in school. Are our cities as prepared for this situation as they are to host two- or three-day conferences, to receive international leaders, or to celebrate Armed Forces Day? Do our cities use more resources for those events than for promoting integral childhood development and caregivers' well-being? Doesn't that generate a social model? Are we aware of having chosen it?

For institutions and companies in a territory where the logistics of 300 flights a day are organized in many cities, articulating a network of natural spaces along strategic routes through the city should not be an insurmountable difficulty. Some may argue that the profits from an airport's activity provide sufficient economic benefits to finance its logistics, and that, in that sense, the efforts necessary to encourage play in the city are not comparable. I would ask those people to try to imagine the benefits, within a broader scope of time, generated by comprehensive childhood development, regardless of social class or family situation – the collective gain that a successful work-life balance can provide. We should also bear in mind the investment of resources that goes on in many cities for activities that are only indirectly (as opposed to directly) productive: for example, the planting and maintenance of decorative flower beds. If measured by itself, the activity is a pure consumer of resources; yet it contributes to improving tourism, investment figures, and the number of companies interested in opening a local office. Building the caring city, as we will see later, involves calculating the profitability of both productive and non-productive activities, considering broader time frames, direct and indirect benefits, and how we distribute rights and privileges among our citizens.

Let's look at the proposal based on a more symmetrical and horizontal idea of love, in Amy Mullin's terms. If we assume that minors can act with co-responsibility towards their surroundings, and that those of us who care for them can take pleasure from their play, similar to theirs, then it is worth rethinking some of the new characteristics of playgrounds:

• By ensuring a certain proximity or density of these small pixel gardens, we could guarantee sequences of stimuli that would articulate routes, from the point of view of play, which would be compatible with other needs on the part of families, caregivers, friends and playmates.

• Situating them in places that are significant to the community, we contribute to helping children participate in their construction. Tonucci says something similar: children may be young, but they are still citizens, who should be asked for some level of collaboration and responsibility, in accordance with their abilities. When we build playgrounds in front of heritage and institutional buildings, in front of places that are significant or useful to the community, are we not encouraging co-responsibility for the public sphere? Let's look back at our example from Candem: children remember their significant experiences associated with places much more than the places themselves. If we begin offering them memorable stimuli in connection with things we appreciate and wish to preserve, we will be forming an initial connection, a first memory, a first sense of belonging.

• Although it's fantastic to go to playgrounds on weekends when you have nothing to do, that isn't always possible. Incorporating play stimuli into places where adults have obligations, where they need to run an errand, or to make it easier for them to take care of other needs, would reinforce in children that sense of co-responsibility towards their families, first, and towards other citizens second, which could contribute to a policy of true conciliation. People were often surprised at how well behaved my two-year-old son was when I took him to professional meetings; what they didn't know (although I have to admit some of them later discovered my secret) was that, after each meeting, we systematically looked for a public fountain, took off our shoes and splashed around together. I think my son was able to wait calmly for the end of the meetings because he knew that we would have a moment of fun together afterward, which we enjoyed immensely.

• In a truly symmetrical view of the benefits of care, there should be fun on a playground for everyone involved. Not without reason, Robin Moore (1989) thinks of parks as places for family stimulation. Walking barefoot in the sand has countless benefits for adults; imagine how many more it would have after standing in line, rushing around, and being made to wait. In reality, if it were implemented, this proposal for pixel gardens would not only form a network of parks, but also a network of spaces to combat stress and to support urban biodiversity. As we will see later, the agenda of care converges with many other needs in today's cities.

• Introducing a wheat field into the city, where you can play hide-and-seek, for example, or squares of grass, or fruit trees, or ponds full of fish, would support open activities where children can take the initiative: they can decide how to play, uncover meaning, show us what to do. This prepares them for one of the proposals Tonucci put forward (2015): the active participation of children in city planning. Otherwise, I think we can only talk about democracy with a lowercase "d" and as an objective that will never be fully achieved in the city.

• This same policy of reintroducing small pixels of nature into the city could be applied to places specifically intended for children's play, like school playgrounds, while involving the neighborhood in their maintenance. Superstudio, the team of Italian architects who practiced in the 1970s, seen by some as radical and by others as utopian, proposed as a revolutionary act the creation of a collage that showed an endless stretch of pavement from which a small portion had been removed to reveal a patch of natural ground on which a family was enjoying themselves. Children have an enormous lack of contact with nature. The group Emplázate describes how, at more than one school, they have seen children lining up to stick a shovel into a hole in the only unpaved section of the playground just to feel the pleasure of the dirt between their fingers. At the same time, this deficit can be extended to include most citizens, and caring for a shared heritage among neighbors and students is what generates, precisely, the construct of that shared heritage.

CHAPTER 2 RAISED SIDEWALKS VERSUS MOBILITY A LA CARTE

Vehicles in cities

In compliance with the agreements reached at the Paris Summit in 2015, 145 Spanish cities with more than 50,000 inhabitants will be obliged to introduce a low-emissions area proportional to the size of their population by 2023. The hope is that this will result in a 50% decrease in the number of vehicles in circulation in each city. The objectives that can be achieved through these measures are multiple (Estevan and Sanz, 1996):

• Promoting a more efficient model of energy consumption, less dependent on oil – the main source of the energy consumed by cars – given that cars are the means of transportation that consumes the most energy per person transported and per kilometer travelled (whether the calculation is based on maximum occupancy rates or actual occupancy rates). Because private vehicles are the most inefficient means of transportation (their energy consumption is almost double that of commuter trains and subways and four times that of buses[10]), decreasing their presence compared to other means of transportation is the best way to reduce impacts on a global scale:

limiting the effects of climate change and the impacts related to obtaining and distributing energy.

• Reducing pollution in cities and, with it, the negative effects on the health of people and other living beings: including the irritation of eyes, mucous membranes and lungs, an increase in overall mortality and deaths as a result of respiratory diseases and heart disease, the loss of lung function, the risk of lung cancer and, according to recent research, a reduction in cognitive capacity, intellectual abilities and memory, and the acceleration in the onset of neurological diseases. This reduction is potentially significant, considering that cars are responsible for 80% of the NO_2 emissions from traffic and 60% of particle emissions, and that 18 million people in the Spanish state live in places with polluted air.

• Offering special protection for vulnerable communities, which are more impacted by the effects of pollution; older people, minors and asthmatics or people with respiratory problems are the most sensitive.

• Increasing the urban surface dedicated to uses other than parking and circulation, and recovering streets as places for meeting and socializing. Private vehicles remain parked, on average, for 90% of the day (between 20 and 22 hours), and it is the means of transport that occupies the most space during travel (90 times more than travel by subway and 20 times more than travel by bus or streetcar). As a result, the urban area dedicated to automobiles is between 20% and 30% of the total, reaching percentages as high as 40% in newly built developments. This proportion of occupied urban space is divided between areas for parking and areas for vehicle circulation.

10 Including the consumption associated with the manufacture of the vehicle, the construction of associated infrastructure and its maintenance.

• Reducing traffic accidents and mitigating the leading cause of death in young people. Accidents are the main cause of death in people under 39 years of age and the fifth cause (behind heart disease, malignant neoplasms, and respiratory and digestive diseases) for the population as a whole. This significant accident rate has a serious urban impact: more than half of all accidents occur in cities. Of the total number of people injured in traffic accidents, 50% are injured in cities; the figures for people hit by cars are similar. Most motorcycle accidents take place in urban areas: 76% of the total.

• Improving travel times and eliminating traffic jams. Delays in travel times have a fundamental impact on work-life balance, on mood and on health, in addition to their economic impact because they result in a loss of hours for production and commerce. Moreover, cars have a negative effect on public transportation and on non-motorized means of transportation. In the competition for limited public space, the biggest loser is the public bus system: the quality of its service suffers, and significant public investment is required to keep it running. In this unfair competition, the bus loses potential passengers who opt for private vehicles (perpetuating the problem) or other means of transportation.

• Noise reduction. 80% of urban noise comes from road traffic. Streetcars generate 46 times less noise than cars, and buses 11 times less noise than the equivalent number of cars. "According to the European Union, 74% of Spain's residents are exposed to sound levels above 55 decibels caused by traffic,"[11] and "two out of three residents of medium-sized or large Spanish cities live in an acoustic environment that is broadly considered to be unacceptable".[12] This impact is not limited to direct effects, such as distress, problems with communication and attention, or sleep disorders, but also

11 https://www.ecologistasenaccion.org/9846/los-problemas-del-coche-2/#nb34-8
12 Ibid.

encompasses the effects of prolonged exposure: chronic fatigue, insomnia, heart disease, immune system disorders, anxiety, depression, irritability, nausea, headaches, and behavioral changes including hostility, irritability, aggressiveness, and social withdrawal.

• Increasing the use of low-impact vehicles. The overuse of cars, with their expansion in urban areas in recent decades, has also caused an inhibition of non-motorized transport. Pedestrians and cyclists are pushed out of a hostile city – a city designed for cars, without spaces or facilities for walking or riding bicycles, in which the regime of fear (of being run over) associated with cars and the pollution they produce combine to dissuade pedestrians and cyclists.

All these points can result in a more caring city, but, in addition to those goals, we can pursue an improvement in the development of care-related activities carried out by the city's residents by addressing mobility. Urban mobility has specific features that are characteristic of cities. In the study "Who travels by car in London and for what purpose?" we see how car use increases as people age until it reaches a peak in users between 40 and 49, who make an average of 1.16 trips per day in a private vehicle. This age coincides largely with the stage of life in which most families in the UK have young or teenage children and elderly dependents. This link between mobility and care is confirmed by the same report, which describes how adults caring for households that contain at least one child make an average of 0.93 trips, compared to the 0.58 trips made by adults at the head of households with no children.

Mobility, additionally, has its own gender gap: according to the same report, men make more trips than women (0.83 trips a day for men, compared to 0.65 for women). Mobility also shows differences in terms of social class and purchasing power: families that earn more money use cars more often. This rule holds true for family income levels of up to £75,000; beginning from this amount, the number of car trips per family evens out.

These final points support the adoption of mobility formulas not centered on private vehicles. To begin with, because we will save energy, we will combat climate change, we will reduce pollution, noise and accidents; we will protect the health of the most vulnerable communities, we will recover space for socialization; we will have more efficient travel times and we will be able to make use of bicycles or scooters in much safer, healthier and more enjoyable ways. For those who find these arguments insufficient, there are a few more related to social cohesion: in a city where mobility is not centered on private vehicles, it is less likely that educational and leisure options will diverge according to social class. Getting to piano lessons, French lessons or tennis classes during the week is much more difficult for families with fewer resources, but easy access from home to these activities would make them available to more people. A new mobility model would also contribute to supporting the work-life balance and reducing the gender gap. That is why I think it is essential for us, as a society, not to miss the great opportunity presented by the implementation of these low-emission zones by limiting our actions to merely cutting back on vehicle traffic. We should take advantage of this momentum to commit to a new model of mobility and public space.

Transforming Mobility

The change in mobility we believe needs to be adopted starts from an important foundation: pedestrians should be the main users of public space, while drivers of private vehicles should feel that they are temporarily invading a public space that does not belong to them. This approach can be seen in the work of Hans Monderman (1945-2008) and his disciples, who coined the expression "shared space". This concept encompasses projects that aim to minimize the demarcations between vehicular traffic and pedestrians, often eliminating elements like curbs, surface road markings, traffic signs or traffic lights. Monderman found that traffic efficiency and safety improve when streets and the surrounding public spaces are redesigned to encourage every person to negotiate their movement directly with others. Monderman was convinced that, for at least several generations, motorized traffic will continue to be an essential feature of European economies and the spatial fabric of its cities. But this type of traffic would gradually tend to decrease and even disappear from urban centers. Monderman helped many cities design spaces suited to this transition, which he considered a technical and political goal. In this context, he reviewed the technologies and practices for designing streets and recommended the elimination of many elements that he considered negative or counterproductive (Moody and Melia, 2014). One of Monderman's best-known achievements is the Dutch district of Woonerf, or the Living Street project, which originated from a largely unplanned citizens' initiative in Delft in 1968.

In the tradition of shared space, another example worth mentioning is Exhibition Road, a street in South Kensington, London. The street's name came from the Great Exhibition of 1851, which was held at the northern end of Hyde Park. It is the central element of an area known as Albertopolis and provides access to many institutions of national importance, including the Victoria and Albert Museum, the Science Museum, the Natural History Museum (incorporating the former Geological Museum), the Royal Geographical Society, Imperial College London, Pepperdine University Abroad, and Jagiellonian University Abroad. The London Goethe Institute and the Church of Jesus Christ of Latter-day Saints are also located on Exhibition Road.

In 2003, a design competition was organized by the Royal Borough of Kensington and Chelsea to improve the street's design and reflect its cultural importance. The winning proposal was submitted by the architectural firm Dixon and Jones with a shared space scheme for the main thoroughfare and surrounding streets that would give pedestrians a higher priority, while allowing some vehicle traffic at reduced speeds. The project also aimed to improve the artistic and architectural quality of the urban landscape, drawing clear inspiration from Gordon Cullen's concept of a Townscape. The design was completed before the 2012 London Olympics, and since then it has made a significant contribution to urban quality.

What these interventions share is that they have led to a reduction in speed, car traffic, and accidents and an increase in environmental quality based on three mechanisms: the conscious defense of public space as a shared territory in which vehicles are not given priority; mediation in the conflicts that arise between citizens in the use of public space; and giving them back the responsibility over their own actions (Karndacharuk et al., 2014). Undoubtedly, this is the path that should be universalized.

The conditions under which our cities will be transformed to comply with the Paris agreements should follow this shared space philosophy. As I see it, however, it should be updated or adapted to suit a situation that is somewhat different from what Monderman observed during his work. I would cite three essential differences.

• The confirmation of the effects of climate change. When Monderman was practicing, this finding was not as evident, nor was there such widespread social consensus around the need to mitigate its effects. I believe that shared space today should contribute to greening cities, one of the few measures that have proven effective in preventing temperature rise.

• The widespread implementation of low emission areas in Europe for the 2023 horizon is initially incompatible with completely redeveloping all the streets that will be affected. European governments would not be able to afford the investment of resources, money and energy that would be required to treat all the streets in the low emission areas like Exhibition Road. We need systems for transforming public space that are compatible with the surface urbanization of many existing neighborhoods and streets.

• Shared spaces have already been implemented and evaluated in several cities and, although they yield extraordinary results in promoting diversity, identity, environmental quality and civility, they generate profiles of more vulnerable users (people with impaired vision, the elderly, and children) whose needs we must continue working to address.

In that regard, at the architecture studio I direct we been developed various proposals for urban space that are especially relevant today. In 2005, we were invited to participate in a competition to remodel the boulevard in the Ensanche de Vallecas, then under construction (Chinchilla, 2004: 56). The boulevard is 50 meters wide and, at the time, aligning ourselves with expert opinions like Hans Monderman's, we envisioned a reduction in vehicle traffic. Thus, we proposed dividing the more than 50-meter-wide boulevard into more than 10 lanes, separated by bands of landscaping. These strips of landscape and the location of the lanes closest to the left (west) and the right (east) sides, or to the center of the old road, generated different situations in terms of sunlight, ventilation and habitability. Indicators such as lights of different colors or pieces of flexible urban furniture would let the city council or neighborhood communities change the uses for each lane. Some of the lanes used for traffic during peak hours on weekdays would be allocated for pedestrians, bicycles, sports or play areas aimed at specific ages. The lanes with the best sunlight, temperatures and humidity levels at each moment were destined for non-vehicular use. The cars were left with the least conditioned lane in each season.

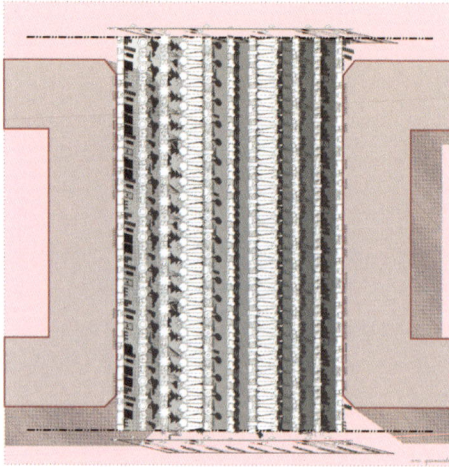

Boulevard in the Ensanche de Vallecas.
Channel distribution on the boulevard
©Izaskun Chinchilla Architects.

For this competition we used the metaphor of the remote control:
just like we can choose between different channels on the television,
we could decide what use would correspond to each lane. The
concept of governance would then take on a much more active
meaning. It would not be limited, as is the case in many cities
today, to maintenance work and to ensuring basic compliance
with laws and regulations. Instead, it would imply the articulation
of a permanent negotiation on the use of space, similar to the one
Monderman proposed, in which citizens, in addition to operating
individually, might do so as part of associations or institutions or by
contributing to participatory mechanisms for management.

In this book, we want to propose a combination of both formulas,
even alternating with pedestrianizations that are sometimes
permanent and sometimes temporary or reversible, generating a

DESCRIPCIÓN DE LOS CANALES PAISAJÍSTICOS QUE SECUNDARÍAN LOS CARRILES DE TRÁNSITO DE LA PROPUESTA CUANDO PRIMARA EL MECANISMO DE COMPENSACIÓN.

CANAL 1 OFRECE UNA INTERFAZ ADECUADA ENTRE ESPACIO PÚBLICO Y PRIVADO.

CANAL 2 OFRECE UNA PROTECCIÓN ESPECIALMENTE ADECUADA PARA VERANO.

CANAL 3 OFRECE UNA PROTECCIÓN ESPECIALMENTE ADECUADA PARA VERANO.

CANAL 4 OFRECE UNA PROTECCIÓN ESPECIALMENTE ADECUADA PARA DÍAS CON EXCESO DE RADIACIÓN SOLAR O CON LLUVIA EN DÍA TEMPLADO.

CANAL 5 OFRECE UNA PROTECCIÓN ESPECIALMENTE ADECUADA PARA PRIMAVERA.

CANAL 6 OFRECE UNA PROTECCIÓN ESPECIALMENTE ADECUADA PARA ENTRETIEMPO.

CANAL 7 OFRECE UNA PROTECCIÓN ESPECIALMENTE ADECUADA PARA OTOÑO.

CANAL 8 OFRECE UNA PROTECCIÓN ESPECIALMENTE ADECUADA PARA DÍAS DE LLUVIA O TARDES DE OTOÑO CON EXCESO DE RADIACIÓN.

CANAL 9 OFRECE UNA PROTECCIÓN ESPECIALMENTE ADECUADA PARA INVIERNO.

CANAL 10 OFRECE UNA PROTECCIÓN ESPECIALMENTE ADECUADA PARA INVIERNO.

CANAL 11 OFRECE UNA INTERFAZ ADECUADA ENTRE ESPACIO PÚBLICO Y PRIVADO

Boulevard in the Ensanche de Vallecas. Description of the landscape channels ©Izaskun Chinchilla Architects.

set of urban actions that could have a more extensive and universal application for the large number of cities that will soon implement low emission areas and the different conditions of the spaces in those cities. The challenge of complying with the Paris agreements from 2015 can support the redevelopment of many roads, which might make Monderman's idea of shared space possible and which, like in the case of Exhibition Road, requires a considerable economic investment. What is desirable is for that collective and international awareness in the fight against climate change to translate into financing the improvement of public space. But if that investment is not large enough to redevelop all the affected streets (remove surface finishes, permanently reorganize traffic, or reconfigure pavements and furniture) we could put alternative plans into place that provide for a temporary modification of the use of public space and an incorporation of green elements with a smaller investment. Many wishes have been expressed for public space, but from a technical point of view, I maintain that it is possible and desirable to combine them. The width, location and traffic levels for each street are so varied that it would be desirable and realistic to be able to apply one or more of these strategies. Even large avenues or boulevards admit and demand the combination of these principles in sections with different characteristics and different levels of consolidation.

Our à la carte traffic strategy does not require the redevelopment of roads and squares. In fact, one of the reasons we proposed this strategy was that the boulevard in the Ensanche de Vallecas was already partially developed when we were invited to join the competition. The à la carte traffic strategy was based exclusively on permanent and adaptable elements of signage. It would be compatible with a gradual redevelopment strategy, in which the pavement could be removed in stages, funded by incremental investments, if necessary.

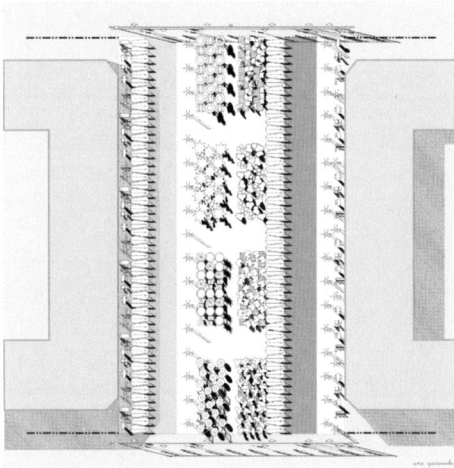

Boulevard in the Ensanche de Vallecas. Distribution of channels on the boulevard ©Izaskun Chinchilla Architects.

Since we know that it is hard to imagine this new city and its transformation process, we will try to describe how these strategies might be combined on a wide avenue or boulevard based on our cities' current needs. Let's start by assuming that, at least in a large portion of that public space, the implementation of a shared space following Monderman's principles is viable: we would opt for a continuous pavement that is especially pleasant for pedestrians, bicycles, skateboards and scooters, and which is attractive from and urban perspective. According to Monderman's logic, the use of permanent signage on the pavement to guide traffic should be avoided. But, as we said earlier, the investments aimed to curb the effects of climate change should be associated with an increase in and densification of green areas in the city. The interventions carried out by Monderman's followers don't contain many green spaces, but there are many traffic islands to prevent vehicle circulation, in addition to the presence of urban furniture, so not all the space

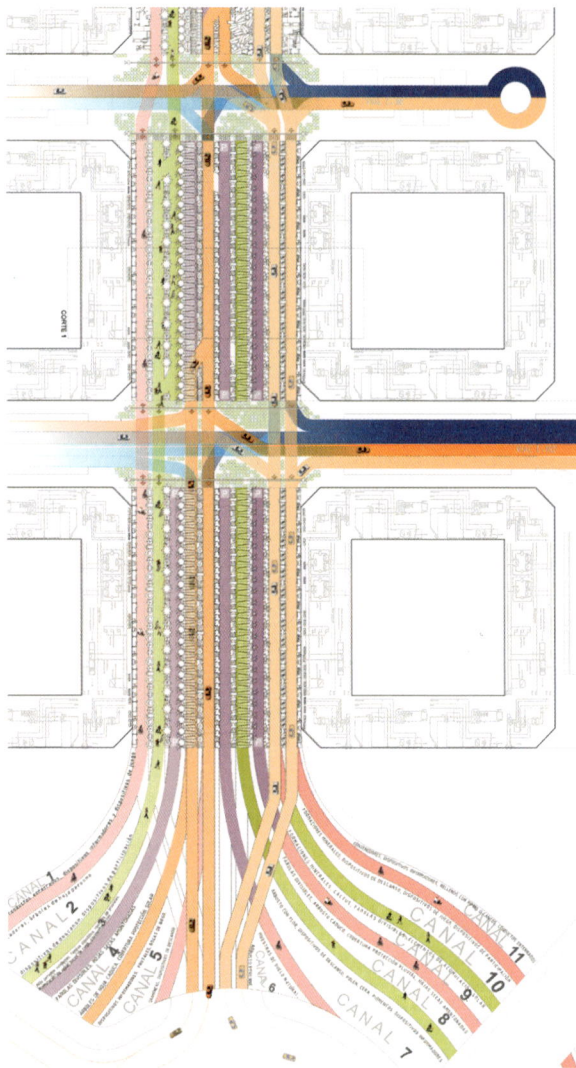

Boulevard in the Ensanche de Vallecas. Detail of the overview in plan ©Izaskun Chinchilla Architects.

is allocated to paved roads. However, the designs aim to maintain transparency and visibility in order to prevent vehicles from hitting pedestrians coming out from behind an obstacle that is blocking their view. This logic of use is compatible with replanting street trees, so long as around the trees, like around the street furniture, there is a change of pavement that prevents vehicles from invading the area and allows pedestrians to emerge from behind the trees onto a pedestrian area that is still safe for them.

The combination of shared spaces with islands of green is possible in streets that have a certain width and in squares. If we assume that there might not be enough budget for a complete redevelopment of a section of a large avenue or urban area, mobile elements could be incorporated into the areas paved with traditional asphalt that would restrict traffic during certain hours of the day, specifically after the evening rush hour and before the morning rush hour, and on weekends. These spaces could be used for collective yoga classes, tai chi or Pilates (as is the case in public parks such as Lumpini Park in Bangkok), for sports, or for the installation of small tents or temporary architectural elements for workshops, health care visits or mobile libraries. These elements intended to temporarily rearrange the uses of public space should be designed using a language that avoids a connotation of prohibition and contributes to environmental quality; for example, mobile planters would be more suitable than security fences.

Streets need to be subject to programming, just like museums, cultural centers or sports centers can be. The programming of workshops and activities organized by municipal bodies should be extended into public space: the usual urban landscape should include sports, culture, music, plays, puppet shows, and performances. It can also provide the opportunity to bring citizens into closer contact with health care services (blood drives and various primary care services are already carried out using mobile units). The offer can be combined with private participation and with the extension of commercial activities into public space. This programming can and should be aimed at reducing the presence of private vehicles, promoting a work-life balance, and making sure the activities associated with childcare and caring for dependents can take place close to people's homes.

These forms of urbanization, in which uses are itinerant to some degree, would make it possible to recover types of vegetation that are seldom used in public spaces today, such as evergreen trees, which are generally avoided because they generate too much shade in winter.

These three design guidelines – the use of mobile elements in the city, the use of intelligent signage, and the programming of public space – present an enormous challenge for municipal administrations and for citizens because they depend on a new area of activity: a much more proactive governance. Until now, municipal intervention in the city consisted of planning, investing and executing its urban development projects. The responsibility for subsequent maintenance would remain, but there was no need for an exercise of active governance. The challenges of this new mobility demand that administration engage in an ongoing administration of the built city. This is happening successfully in cities like Bogotá.

The identification of governance as an emerging need opens up a new field of opportunities for collaboration – and not just between the public and private sectors. It also makes room for promotion: on the part of municipal policy or citizen associations. Governance offers the possibility for neighborhood parents to join together to organize activities related to sports, education, culture, etc., contributing to the construction of social capital in the sense it has been used by Putnam.

CHAPTER 3 WHITE ARROWS VERSUS SHARED PATTERNS

Architecture and the Meandering Paths through Airports

I am a regular user of Stansted Airport, having traveled there every week for almost nine months of the year over the last decade. The building was completed in 1991, a few years before I started at architecture school, and it was one of the first buildings that I went to visit on the recommendation of my teachers when I was a young student. Thus, I have witnessed its evolution over the last 25 years. On my first visit, Stansted Airport was fabulous for the user in terms of being able to navigate intuitively. The space was rectangular in plan with hardly any interior partitions. When they were necessary, they were always of a moderate height, under four meters, which, given the great height of the interior space (over 14 meters) never hindered the view of the roof structure. This made it possible to perceive the continuity of the building above the partitions. Additionally, the perimeter enclosure consisted of a curtain wall and a series of tree-like pillars. The way the elements were organized meant that, upon entering the space, the check-in counters, the security control, and the airplanes were all readily visible. The rectangular floor plan was very clear, and the route any traveler needed to follow coincided with the short side, the shortest distance. It was very easy to learn your way around, even for an unseasoned traveler. Upon entering you could see where the planes were, and you knew that was where you needed to go. From the beginning, it was clear that you would need to pass through two filters: one for baggage drop and check-in; and one for security. The transparency and openness of the space helped users to understand, in advance, the route they would need to follow (Powell et al., 1992).

Stansted Airport combined two orientation mechanisms that we might associate with two types of transparency, following the classification offered by Rowe and Slutzky.[13] On the one hand, there was a literal transparency: the absence of interior partitions and the glass around the entire perimeter façade made it possible for travelers to actually see the planes they were heading toward, as well as the check-in counters and the security area in front of them. This was combined with a "phenomenal transparency" to which the architectural structure itself contributed. To explain this second type of transparency, detected by Rowe and Slutzky, I have often used the authors' same examples, based on Cubist painting. The students begin to see that, without a literal transparent surface, people can still understand what comes next if they can recognize a structure, a series, or a sequence. But the clearest example for students, judging from years of teaching, is a train: if you know that a train has a total of eight cars and that you're in car number three, you can understand that there are two cars ahead of you and five behind you without needing to see them, literally, through a transparent pane of glass. The original Stansted also offered that phenomenal transparency. In some places, the partitions, although low, prevented you from

13 In 1967, two members of the Texas Rangers, founded at the University of Austin, Texas, wrote a book on transparency, *Transparency* (1993). Colin Rowe, an architectural historian and theorist, and Robert Slutzky, an abstract painter who was extraordinarily critical of the International Movement, explored different forms of transparency that can help us to understand Stansted's early virtues and subsequent decline.

actually seeing what was behind them, but you never lost sight of the larger view of the structure of the tree pillars and the roof. As a result, you could always tell how far the building continued and in what direction, and since travelers knew they needed to head toward its longest façade, they could rely on a permanent guide.

Over time, and as the commercial expectations for airports have grown, Stansted Airport has changed radically. What used to be a short straight path, with the destination literally in sight or with the possibility of easily anticipating where it would be, has become a convoluted route that has tripled in length and has become a meandering maze in order to ensure users pass through as many stores as possible. The space, even for a regular traveler, is no longer intuitive. From the entrances on one side, the check-in counters are hidden behind a Burger King and several coffee shops. The security control is located at the end of the long side, at just one end, and after passing through it, you have to walk more than 300 meters in a zig-zagging route boxed in between shops and restaurants, with views only of the display windows and commercial offerings. Wayfinding signs have been incorporated because, without them, it is impossible to use your intuition to get to your gate.

I'm often surprised at the fact that travelers who have missed a flight because of the excessive time it takes between checking in and arriving at the gate haven't sued the airport for not enabling the shortest and most direct route possible. I wonder at what point we citizens docilely accepted the obligation of arriving at the airport with enough time to walk through all the shops – in other words, when we gave up on the fact that our right to move efficiently comes before the airport's commercial interests. In a society that knows its rights, I firmly believe that the route to a plane should be the shortest and clearest possible path, prioritizing the rights of those who have limited time, those who may have mobility difficulties, or who may find the airport a stressful experience that can only be improved by clarity and brevity. Shops and restaurants should be part of an alternative route that can be taken by whomever voluntarily decides to do so. Unfortunately, Stansted is not an isolated case; in airport itineraries, productive interests have prevailed and, once again, it has happened without any real debate about the de facto suppression of rights that it implies.

In the previous case, the wayfinding operates in a somewhat perverse way. It is a palliative solution that substitutes a much more advantageous layout: configuring a space in which the organization is regulated by intuition and cognitive accessibility (O'Connor, 2019). The wayfinding techniques applied at Stansted airport, as in many others, function based on the assumption that everyone who intends to get on a plane must have specific intellectual abilities and potential for mobility – or, if they don't, they will receive assistance. Minors, people with reduced mobility, people with intellectual disabilities, or citizens of a certain age need special assistance or accompaniment at the airport. They are even considered, implicitly, to be outside the norm of airport users. But people who need special assistance are not the only ones who suffer the inconveniences of organizing a space like an airport in an unintuitive way to prioritize commercial interests. The harmful effects are transferred to all users in the form of stress and sometimes even a missed flight, which could be avoided.

That is why it is important to avoid transferring this navigation model onto the city and onto the public space that belongs to everyone. Signaling or wayfinding techniques, among which I include the use of GPS, cannot and should not replace the kind of good planning that turns the city into a territory that is cognitively accessible and intuitive, and that recognizes the reduction of stress and the incitement of socialization as a shared goal. As we have seen in the case of Stansted, the implementation of these palliative orientation measures has many detrimental effects: on the one hand, it segregates citizens who find signage accessible from those who do not. For people who don't speak the language, who can't see the signs correctly or cannot interpret them, the right to use the city, or a public facility within it, is undermined. Digital tools generate this same gap: for anyone who doesn't have a cell phone, who doesn't know how to use certain applications, or for whom a digital application isn't inclusive (because it isn't available in their language, or because their vision or hearing is impaired), the city turns them into dependents or second-class citizens, into exceptions among the "natural" users of a facility. On the other hand, among those for whom the signage is accessible, it generates a new need: that of paying permanent and monographic attention to it, significantly increasing stress levels and the amount of time invested.

And it is very important to realize that by protecting the interests of citizens for whom the signage is not accessible – groups that, a priori, may seem to be in the minority – it creates a better user experience for the population as a whole. A city that is easy to navigate is one that does not contribute to stress, and one that people will remember as a place it would be nice to visit again, or as an attractive place to live. And I would wager that how navigation is organized in the city can also contribute to the construction of identity or add to the benefits of what has come to be called placemaking. Accessibility impacts the sociability of the city. An inaccessible city is a city that also hinders sociability (Schneekloth et al., 1995). Naturally, the ease of navigation is part of urbanism, of the first stages of planning. Citizens will be able to identify this phenomenal transparency, to return to the terms we used earlier (Rowe and Slutzky, 1997), in cities with an urban structure that is easy to recognize and, therefore, predictable. However, there are many cities in which the geometric layout is far from straightforward, but which are still very pleasant for their inhabitants. Classic authors who have studied these cities, such as Kevin Lynch (2018) or Camillo Sitte (2013), have attributed this warmth to the widespread presence of recognizable public spaces (squares) and of heritage architecture that provides landmarks, and to the artistic and compositional quality of the urban elements. Thus, when we inherit a city whose main layout lacks the clarity to support navigation, we can understand that it will be difficult to change that condition within a short period of time. But, in the medium term, we can aim to introduce those articulating public spaces, to set up landmarks and, even within a shorter time horizon, to increase the compositional and artistic quality of the environment, an idea that we will look to develop in the following section.

The Recognition and Use of Shared Patterns in Architecture

In 2017, we participated in a competition for the redevelopment of the Los Jardinillos square and park in Palencia, Spain. The particularities of the square included that it housed the exit from the city's only train station and was located at a certain distance from the city center. As a result, we felt that it could act as an important entrance to the city and as the starting point for a series of urban itineraries that would link the station with the city's main facilities, urban landmarks, and heritage buildings. To mark these routes, we proposed using a series of motifs or patterns based on architectural elements from the city and the province. We selected a series of heritage buildings and "extracted" a geometric figure or representative element from them, which, through-repetition or combination, was turned into a pattern. These patterns were sometimes used on the pavement, as a more or less continuous covering; other times they were reproduced only on street corners, on urban furniture, or on stand-alone elements. What this aimed to achieve was to accompany citizens and visitors on their way toward the buildings that had served as a point of reference in their creation.

The use of a pattern as a resource to serve as a guide is founded on how perception operates in the city and, in general, in complex

Escuela del Barrio de la Puebla • C
Palencia
1600m

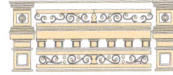

Palacio de la Dip. provincial • F
Palencia
650m

Villa romana La Olmeda • A
Pedrosa de la Vega
58km

Colegio de Villandrando • D
Palencia
700m

Casa de los Sres. García Germán • G
Palencia
350m

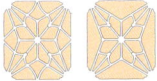

Catedral de San Antolín • B
Palencia
650m

Plaza de Abastos • E
Palencia 650m

Casa Constitucional • H
Becerril de Campos
15km

Shared Patterns (Palencia). References for the patterns.
©Izaskun Chinchilla Architects.

contexts. There is a consensus, today, that pattern recognition is central to the cognitive processes and intelligent responses that are the foundation for many human activities. Pattern recognition has a close connection to the senses, to memory and to culture, and it is one of the most important windows onto many of the activities of human psychology. Pattern recognition can be considered the bedrock of any perceptual process, and it is dependent on our prior knowledge and experience. Generally speaking, pattern recognition refers to the process by which we compare what we perceive (stimulus) with information that we already have in our memories. This process of comparison helps us situate a new stimulus within categories we already recognize. Thus, the stimulus is dependent on one's own knowledge and memory. Without deploying knowledge and experience, human beings cannot understand meanings or even recognize objects. This process by which we distinguish a pattern and identify what it means is called "pattern recognition" (Wang, 2002).

Current cognitive theory proposes three methods for pattern recognition: template matching, prototype matching, and feature analysis. We will describe them briefly here, because we believe they are relevant to understanding how people perceive the city, and they informed the goals and articulation of our proposal for marking routes through the city using patterns. After describing the methods, we will briefly reflect on whether each of them can be identified as a so-called "bottom-up" or "top-down" process. A perception process is said to occur from the top down when it mainly uses information that is already stored in our memory. In keeping with these methods, we intuit or "reconstruct" what we are seeing based on prior experience (Gregory, 2005). In bottom-up methods, the driver of the comprehension process is the stimulus or the data we are perceiving. These methods are also known as "ecological" because the environment plays a key role in them (Reed, 1988).

The template method implies that we store "mini copies" of complete elements in our long-term memory, which serve to define an object or category. In the case of the city, one of these categories might be a street. Following this method, our memories would contain complete street models, and we would attempt to identify our surroundings in an urban environment by using one of the streets that we have stored away. To do this, the information is encoded, compared and contrasted until we find the template that best corresponds to the new stimulus. The template theory has some limitations: receivers need to have stored a complete template in their memory before they can recognize a pattern. Thus, this theory not only places decisive relevance on memory, but also introduces a certain rigidity or lack of flexibility into the recognition process (Wang, 2002).

The second theory is the prototype theory, which argues that memory does not store templates, which are then compared one by one with a new stimulus. Instead of an internalized copy of a pattern, the prototype represents the set of attributes belonging to a category of objects – that is, the abstract characteristics of all the individuals that are part of that category or species (Wang, 2002). In programming, the example of a fork is often used: the prototype of a fork would be an elongated object with an approximate width-to-length ratio of 1/20, ending in a series of points (three or four) at one end, and a handle or grippable element at the other. The prototype does not account for specific aspects like material (metal, plastic), shine, curvature or ornamentation. The prototype is what all forks have in common. The process of recognizing a stimulus will be more efficient because it will only need to be compared with the prototype. Once the stimulus matches a prototype, it is filed away in that item's category. This process is more flexible than template matching, but it has some drawbacks because it is still a top-down process.

The third theory is that of feature analysis. According to this third theory, receivers attempt to match the features of a pattern with the ones stored in their memory, rather than matching a complete template or prototype (Wang, 2002). This is the most flexible of the theories, the one that offers the best results in programming, and the one that works fundamentally from the bottom up.

Our proposal for Palencia was based on developing a series of grids or patterns that could be used in different itineraries and that were inspired by architectural elements from the city and the province, chosen in workshops by the citizens themselves. Working with groups of people of different ages, physical conditions, and cultural origins, we selected a series of heritage buildings from which we

Shared Patterns (Palencia). Perimeter plan of the shared spaces.
©Izaskun Chinchilla Architects.

extracted a geometric figure or representative element that we then turned into a pattern using repetition or combination. The workshops helped us delve not only into the expanded definitions of heritage, but also into the models of perception of patterns in the city, honing in on which features are the most distinctive, appealing and recognizable in certain urban elements.

The patterns are used as motifs on the pavement whenever possible. Their location within the urban fabric directs residents or visitors towards the buildings in question, all of which are heritage buildings. Thus, each pattern acts like a carpet that guides pedestrians in the direction of the selected landmark or heritage building.

In some cases, the prints or patterns could be applied by replacing the pavement (when necessary, for example, to eliminate the raised sidewalks around the park to create a shared space), but often

Shared Patterns (Palencia). Details of adapted pavements.
©Izaskun Chinchilla Architects.

Shared Patterns (Palencia). Details of adapted pavements.
©Izaskun Chinchilla Architects.

Shared Patterns (Palencia). Axonometric drawing of the whole.
©Izaskun Chinchilla Architects.

enough the proposal involved simply using spray paint to create a
carpet leading towards the heritage element. In the rest of the city,
these applications might be continued in the form of a narrow path
or line, or even as an intermittent trail marked by single tiles on
corners or by repeating the pattern on trash cans or street furniture.

Following the theory of feature analysis, patterns can be formed
progressively, based on different element: starting with one simple
component, combining it with another, repeating them, adding a
third, etc. This would make it possible to include a serial or narrative

reading that would help toward interpreting a path by associating it with a sequence in time (if I'm heading in the right direction, it completes the pattern). Today's urban art has proven that it has the resources to support urban routes using narrative, and we believe that these patterns can facilitate citizen navigation in very diverse and sophisticated ways.

This intervention is aimed at restoring the right to intuition in the city – that is, to make navigation simple and clear for inhabitants of all conditions. By also choosing motifs from heritage architecture as "guides" in the city, we aimed to increment the public relevance of this type of architecture, which, as in the case of the Biking to School project, would take on more relevance in collective memory, while helping to articulate the representation of the image of the city. Community participation expands the definitions of heritage in architecture.

This intervention is also considered an instance of what has come to be called placemaking. Placemaking actions aim to improve the habitability of urban space: generating healthier spaces that are more suitable for pedestrians, with more social and cultural activity, more green areas, more identity, more scenic quality, and that promote more well-being and happiness (Palermo and Ponzini, 2015). Community participation in this process is essential, as is aligning with the residents' goals and potentials (Schneekloth, 1995). The proposal for the itineraries using patterns aimed to revitalize marginal and underused streets and improve the pedestrian experience to contribute to the construction and reinforcement of new mobility habits in the city.

CHAPTER 4 BOLLARDS VERSUS LOOSE PARTS URBAN FURNITURE

Bollards: Prohibiting with Objects

There are many authors who have asserted that the urban regulations and laws that govern coexistence in cities have relied too often on prohibition. (McKinnon, 2007; Moroni and Basta, 2013). In his book *El buen salvaje: de urbanitas campesino y ecologistas varios* (1981), Mario Gaviria compiled early 20th-century ordinances from various Spanish cities that may now seem unnecessary (prohibiting things like "shouting out news headlines", or "congretating in front of churches", or "sailing toy boats in public fountains"), surprising ("discharging firearms on Easter Sunday is prohibited" or "carrying transistor radios on public streets is prohibited"), or directly unfair ("pedestrians are prohibited from gathering on sidewalks"). More difficult to classify was the edict issued by the Malaga City Council in 1940, which prohibited pedestrians from walking on the "left" side of sidewalks. The latest Citizen Security Law (known as the "gag order") has been met with protests gathering tens of thousands of participants.

Protests against laws that limit freedom in the city have been common (recall the "It is forbidden to forbid" slogan from 1968), but there are fewer protests against things that have come to be seen as natural in cities: what we will call the prohibitions embedded in objects. Bollards are one example of prohibition embodied in an object. A priori, they tell drivers: "You are not allowed to park on this sidewalk". But the message goes further. If the aim were only to transmit that message, a yellow line on the street would be sufficient. Bollards are more adamant in their implicit communication. They say: "The institution that governs this city does not trust that you will obey this rule and has implemented a system so that your vehicle will be damaged in case of disobedience."

But bollards aren't just talking to drivers. They also send strong messages to pedestrians. An elderly pedestrian who has banged a leg and been guaranteed a conspicuous bruise, or a parent trying to move around the city with a stroller (not to mention a twin stroller) is also receiving a strong message. It sounds something like: "This street has been designed to mediate in an ongoing, bloody conflict between vehicles and institutions. That conflict takes priority over your comfort. The problems this object may generate for you are minor collateral damage." In Monderman's view, bollards, like other traffic signals, perpetuate and reinforce a devastating political message: "The city is planned and governed fundamentally in terms of a dialogue with private vehicles. Less attention is devoted to pedestrians because it is assumed they will be able to adapt to the urban landscape resulting from a design that caters to vehicles."

Bruno Latour calls these objects that affect our performance "quasi-objects", to distinguish them from natural objects and to highlight the fact that they are the result of a long design and manufacturing process in which the decision-making is affected by social content and a program pursuing a particular effect on the collective (Latour, 1993: 55). Latour gives decisive importance to the presence of this type of objects in our living environments and their capacity for implicit persuasion, and he argues that these quasi-objects are so powerful that they shape society, while the political or scientific constructions that have given rise to their existence remain invisible (Latour, 1993: 53).

But let's get back to bollards. Imagine that, before installing the bollards, a political party presented a bill in Parliament defending something like the following: "In public space, priority will be given to the management of the flows of private vehicles. In cases where this requires significant inconvenience for pedestrian traffic, their interests will be sacrificed in favor of the successful management of vehicle traffic." This law would be the subject of extensive debate and would have little chance of being approved with that wording. And yet, bollards invade our sidewalks and shape us as a society: they force us, de facto, to accept this bill, internalizing the idea that vehicles have priority and pedestrians will have to make do. This situation even makes us feel like we have more rights when we're driving than when we're walking.[14] The presence of objects such as bollards has established the hegemony of the vehicle over shared space without anyone ever having convened a debate about it, adapting our lives and our perceptions of the city to the implicit ideologies inherent in these objects.

For Latour, these implicit effects have become immoral and unconstitutional since they shape our lives without ever having been subjected to political dialogue. It is logical that he encourages us to make demands in that regard: "We want the meticulous sorting of quasi-objects to become possible – no longer unofficially and under the table, but officially and in broad daylight" (Latour, 1993: 142). Latour proposes a Parliament of Things in which the balance of shared space can be restored. He would assert that traffic engineers, municipal experts, independent mobility experts, political parties, neighborhood associations, representatives of the elderly, and parent

14 City councils receive many more complaints and protests when something damages a car than when the effects of an obstacle have a direct impact on a person's body.

teacher associations should discuss the design of bollards and the regulations governing their placement, and even their meaning and appropriateness.

Latour, together with other authors such as Michel Callon, systematized this vision in what they called *actor-network theory*, which accepts that social agents can be both human and non-human (bollards, traffic lights, voting boxes, vaccines), calling the former "actors" and the latter "actants". They explain that actors begin the action and, although "if action is limited to what intentional, meaningful humans do, it is hard to see how a hammer, a basket [...], or a tag could act", we need to take into account all the things that make a difference "in the course of some other agent's action" (Latour, 2005: 72). Speedbumps on the road make drivers slow down and, therefore, they are actants. The view of urban furniture from this perspective takes on a new social and political relevance that has a direct relation with the philosophy of care.

Loose Parts Urban Furniture

In 2016, the Madrid City Council convened a design competition called "Bancos para Compartir" [Benches for Sharing], and I had the immense privilege of being a member of the jury. Of the 218 proposals presented, I defended one called "Sienta Madrid" (with little success, unfortunately, because it was eliminated in the first round). The proposal was substantially different from all the others, because, while the other furniture was designed to occupy a fixed position, Sienta Madrid proposed a system of folding chairs made available to rent with a management method similar to that of BiciMad, Madrid's municipal bike rental system. The great advantage was that the citizens could rent a chair and decide where to put it, which way they wanted to face, how many people they wanted to form a group with, and even how far back they wanted to recline.

The proposal was not completely unprecedented. Several parks, such as Hyde Park or Saint James in London, have a chair loan system, as do other cities. The novelty was that this freedom and flexibility extended out into the city. The project brief was not very explicit in defining where the chair dispensers would be installed or the rules for their use; the illustrations on the panels showed "the new benches" in Madrid's Plaza Mayor.

"Sienta Madrid" was a perfect example of a development associated with a different way of understanding governance. While the other benches assumed an understanding of governance in which the city council, in a centralized way, would decide where to situate the benches, Sienta Madrid demanded an implementation based on a dialogue bringing "public and private stakeholders together in collective forums with public agencies to engage in consensus-oriented decision making" (Ansell and Gash, 2008). In other words, it would have required what we call collaborative governance. The installation of the Sienta Madrid system in the Plaza Mayor, the place chosen by the authors for the illustration on their competition panel, would have depended on a collaboration between neighborhood associations, hoteliers on the plaza, Madrid Destino (the municipal organization dedicated to the promotion of culture, tourism and sports in Madrid, which has its offices on the square), the Madrid Chamber of Commerce, the Institutional Commission for Historic, Artistic and Natural Heritage (CHIPAN), the political parties with representation in the City Council, consumer associations, etc. Together, they would have been required to discuss questions such as: Can the chairs be taken outside the perimeter of the square? Or perhaps, should they only move within a delimited area of the interior, avoiding the porches? Should the perimeter be marked? How can we guarantee that the markings won't affect the heritage interpretation of the surroundings? Can the people sitting in the chairs consume food or beverages? Should they be required to have purchased it in a particular place? Should the area for setting up chairs have a Wi-Fi connection? Who will pay for it? Can users of the nearby terraces connect to the Wi-Fi?

"Sienta Madrid" might not be just a case of collaborative governance during its management, but rather an interesting case study for the anthropology of consumption. In contrast with a model in which the institution offers citizens set services for their consumption (in the sense that they decide whether or not to accept the service but cannot alter it), Sienta Madrid proposes an open management model for the final use of the service: citizens are considered *competent* and *proactive* users, who have the ability to reconfigure the use they make of the institutional support, with more room for decision-making, more autonomy, more participation and more responsibility. The terms that I have used to designate this form of conceptualizing users are borrowed from Noam Chomsky (1976: 238). He distinguishes between competence and performance, the former being all the knowledge that a subject acquires about the culture in which he or she lives; whereas performance is an individual decision the subject makes about what and how much knowledge of that competence will be put into practice. When we encourage citizens to decide where to sit or how to use a specific service, we contribute to their competence: they will learn which areas are sunny which aren't, they may learn about the square, and about the reasons and rules that govern how people coexist in it, so consumption won't just be a part of every subject's cultural competence but will also contribute to expanding it. And we're also asserting that the implementation – the rational and emotional act – should be reflexive and individualized, contributing to citizen awareness with each urban interaction.

At this point it is worth reflecting on why the proposal was quickly eliminated by a jury made up mostly of civil servants. Many members of the jury assumed that the proposal was not even worth discussing, that its defects were so evident that everyone could see them. I tried to invite them to engage in a more nuanced reflection: they were rejecting the proposal because it might lead to conflicts. They objected that a group might sit in a driveway, that the business owners with terrace seating might protest, that there might be robberies, or the chairs might be vandalized; all this was the tip of the iceberg of a series of problems whose true magnitude couldn't be predicted. The criteria for their selection were oriented, initially, toward limiting the possibilities of conflict.

This desire to erase conflict from public space has been widely criticized (and here I would highlight the work of the anthropologist Manuel Delgado for his activism and geographical proximity). First, because it disables part of the political meaning of public space, which is the "space for encounters between free and equal people who debate and argue in an open discursive process aimed at mutual understanding and normative self-understanding" (Sahuí, 2000: 20). And, second, because it supposes an illegitimate[15] exercise of power in which the aim is "to dissuade and cajole any dissidence, any capacity for protest or resistance and – also by extension – any use of the street or square deemed inappropriate", resulting in "a cultural and morphological modeling of urban space" on the part of "professional elites who come overwhelmingly from the hegemonic social strata", and which ends with "the mere requisition of the city, its subjugation – through both its planning and its political management – to the territorial interests of the dominant minorities" (Delgado, 2011).

Indeed, the first-round elimination of a proposal like "Sienta Madrid" precludes even beginning the process of dialogue between the different agents cited above and, furthermore, represents an exercise of power that negates the right of, for example, a group of retirees, to occupy the street and adapt it to their preferences – a right that, on the other hand, is granted to the hotel industry, because it

15 Delgado uses the term "pastoral", which he takes from Foucault.

generates profit and because it has been culturally accepted as part of a standardized urban landscape. Again, in this example, we see how there is an assumption on the part of the public authorities that this right should be reserved for the productive uses of the city.

As a result, the administration perpetuates a patriarchal decision-making system (Mitterauer and Sieder, 1982). For the sake of theoretical protection ("avoiding conflict"), a group, historically made up of adult men, university graduates with specialized education, usurps the decision-making capabilities of the people who need or provide care – historically members of other age groups and women. The initial motivation for this appropriation of decision making is the protection of vulnerable individuals, but, in every instance, the intent focused on protection turns into a monopoly over certain benefits (Messerschmidt, 2018) and an objective loss of opportunities on the part of those who were initially being protected (Becker, 1999).

The problem with the fact that projects requiring collaborative governance are almost systematically short-circuited in order to avoid conflict is not only that it perpetuates the interests of one group over the diversity of citizens; it is that, in addition, we avoid working on mechanisms for social dialogue that can only become effective with practice and with the repeated cultivation of trust-building processes (Ansell and Gash, 2007: 563), generating a false image that participation processes are ineffective when what they require is training; in Chomsky's terms, they require the acquisition of a competence on the part of the participants. From a technical point of view, but also from a symbolic and cultural standpoint, citizens are told, from childhood, that "the planning, design and building of *any part* of the environment is so difficult and special that only the gifted few – those with degrees and certificates in planning, engineering, architecture, art, education, behavioural psychology, and so on – can properly solve environmental problems" (Nicholson, 1972: 5-14).

This last statement was written by Simon Nicholson, who developed the so-called theory of loose parts. He asserts that if children are stimulated from an early age to modify their environment by interacting with individual elements (pieces, branches, blocks, water, materials, reflections), the development of creative skills and the capacity for cooperation can be taught almost uniformly to all members of the community. The benches that were announced as the winners of the Benches to Share competition were not loose parts, they were fixed elements; one more example of an education and governance system in which institutions deprive citizens of any responsibility, taking on a kind of tutelage. As a result, their decision-making capacity, the possibility of asserting their particular interest or of participating actively and creatively in the transformation of their environment, is taken away. Sienta Madrid, like other "loose parts" projects, aimed to give back a sense of responsibility to citizens and, with it, their right to transform their environment along with the necessary education to progressively understand the benefits of their actions in a context of coexistence and diverse interests.

If we think about the logic inherent in actor-network theory, introducing furniture conceived as loose parts into public space results in an increase in the possibilities for interaction and mediation. In a setting with high diversity among inhabitants, the possibility of being able to set up a chair wherever you want would transform a closed-off and somewhat deterministic mediation into an open mediation, in which actors would be able make proactive and conscious decisions which would, therefore, necessarily be more thoughtful with respect to the technical and political context. The result would be an urban landscape where social diversity would be given a physical expression: offering a varied repertoire of possibilities for action.

CHAPTER 5 THE POLLUTED CITY VERSUS THE WOODED CITY

Reusing and Regreening Urban Spaces

We mentioned earlier that, following the 2015 Paris agreements, in 2023, 145 Spanish cities of more than 50,000 inhabitants will need to implement a low emission zones proportional to the size of their populations, and that it is hoped that these areas will bring about a 50% decrease in the number of vehicles circulating in each of those cities. This chapter will try to assess whether the implementation of low emission zones can lead to a positive transformation of the city and its spaces beyond merely reducing the presence of cars. In other words, can we make use of the spaces currently occupied by that 50% of vehicles, either parked or in motion?

Potentially, this decrease in traffic could result in an increase in vacant space in the city, both through the reuse of areas currently used for parking – it is worth noting that private vehicles are parked, on average, for 90% of the day (between 20 and 22 hours) – as well as for the reuse of the spaces currently occupied for circulation, which adds up to a combined total of 30% of urban space. If low emission zones will result in a 50% drop in traffic, we can assume that they will free up 15% of urban space. Part of this space should be reoccupied, no doubt, by public transportation and zero impact vehicles like bicycles and scooters. But it is presumable that the implementation of low emission zones could result in freeing up 10% of urban surface.

Let's look at what that horizon might represent in cities like Madrid. The current low emissions zone in Madrid, initially called Madrid Central and later renamed Madrid 360, comprises 472 hectares. According to our approximate measurement, 47.2 hectares now occupied by roads, almost 40% of the area of the Retiro, could be freed up in the heart of Madrid to be reused for other purposes. But the current Madrid 360 only affects the neighborhoods of Palacio, Embajadores, Cortes, Justicia, Universidad and Sol, reaching just 149,718 of the city's 3,700,000 inhabitants. In other words, it affects 4% of the population. Compliance with the Paris agreements would require a much more ambitious approach in terms of the area and population affected.

From a historical and morphological point of view, Madrid has been the object of a series of extensions, of concentric enclosures and consecutive expansions usually associated with the construction of walls (medieval walls, walls of Felipe II, walls of Felipe IV). The current low emissions zone has remained largely within the area outlined by the walls of Felipe IV, built in 1625, not addressing the protection of the Ensanche de Madrid, dating from the mid-19th century, which includes districts such as Salamanca or Chamberí, where there are a large number of facilities, cultural uses, offices and heritage buildings. Our reflections on the caring city would invite the urgent inclusion of this area within the low emission zone. The area would be easy to segregate, since the expansion was historically limited around its perimeter by a road network known as "las rondas" and which currently consists of the Paseo de Reina Victoria and the streets Raimundo Fernández Villaverde, Joaquín Costa, Francisco Silvela and Doctor Esquerdo. The area inside this perimeter, which includes the historic area within the walls of Felipe IV as well as the

19th-century expansion, would add some 2,294 hectares. Taking 10% of this area, which could be converted from spaces reserved for traffic to another use, would be the equivalent of adding two full Retiro parks into the city.

What uses should be given to this "new surface area" in cities? There is one answer that has been garnering increasing social and specialist consensus over the last four years: it should be reserved for green spaces. One of the reasons this response is met with unanimity ties in with the climate emergency, since the restoration of wooded areas is one of the most effective strategies for climate change mitigation (Van Kooten et al., 2002). The reason is well known: trees have the ability to capture carbon dioxide from the atmosphere and become long-term permanent carbon sinks, absorbing a third of global emissions each year. Trees also help contain rainwater runoff, reduce the risk of fires, and contribute to curbing the thermal island effect. There are multiple platforms across the world – such as C40 Cities, Under2 Coalition, the carbonnCenter, and ICLEI (Local Governments for Sustainability) – that aim to support municipal governments in dealing with climate change, promoting, among other measures, the incorporation of new green areas into cities.

Planting trees, by mitigating the consequences of climate change as well as through other direct and indirect effects, also offers important benefits in terms of personal and collective health (Gold, 1976). Their contributions to the availability of drinking water, the reduction of the greenhouse effect and ground-level ozone, and economic growth are all illustrative examples. But, without a doubt, the most beneficial effect of trees has to do with curbing pollution. The stomata in trees' leaves trap nitrogen oxide, ammonia and sulfur dioxide particles while producing oxygen. In an even broader vision of health, focusing not only pathologies but also levels of comfort and emotional wellbeing, exposure to wooded environments has proven to have even greater benefits, as it has been shown to reduce blood pressure and the production of stress hormones, while stimulating the immune system and improving general sensations of wellbeing (Wolf et al., 2020).

The COVID-19 crisis can offer us a deeper understand and help us to recalibrate the true impact of pollution on our health. Authors like Marshall Burke[16] estimate that the sustained reduction in pollution during the two main months of lockdown probably saved the lives of 4,000 children under 5 and 73,000 elderly people over 70 in China alone; in other words, the reduction in pollution saved more lives than the virus itself has officially taken. And yet, we tolerate living with "structural" pollution every day. Sociologists such as Anthony Giddens and Ulrich Beck have analyzed the types of risks assumed by citizens, separating external risks (natural disasters, random accidents) from those derived from the modernization process or from economic activity, the so-called "manufactured risks". (Giddens, 1999). Our tolerance for each of them is different, also because their media treatment and the political debate they incite is different.

"Patients with chronic lung and heart conditions caused or worsened by long-term exposure to air pollution are less able to fight off lung infections and more likely to die,"[17] says Sara de Matteis, associate professor of Occupational and Environmental Medicine at Cagliari University and member of the European Respiratory Society. "By lowering air pollution levels we can help the most vulnerable in their fight against this and any possible future pandemics." "Governments should have tackled chronic air pollution long ago but have prioritised the economy over health," says Sascha Marschang, Acting

16 https://www.forbes.com/sites/jeffmcmahon/2020/03/16/coronavirus-lock- down-may-have-saved-77000-lives-in-china-just-from-pollution-reduction/#5448b42834fe

17 https://www.energylivenews.com/2020/03/23/residents-of-polluted-cities-at-higher-risk-of-coronavirus-infection/

Secretary General of the European Public Health Alliance (EPHA). "Once this crisis is over, policymakers should speed up measures to get dirty vehicles off our roads. Science tells us that epidemics like Covid-19 will occur with increasing frequency. So cleaning up the streets is a basic investment for a healthier future."[18] "COVID has made the invisible visible," says Zoltán Massay-Kosubek of the EPHA.[19]

This book is intended to add to the many voices telling municipal, regional, national and transnational governments that the implementation of low emission zones cannot wait, and that if it is not accompanied by a consistent policy of planting trees and reusing spaces dedicated to traffic as green spaces, we'll only be doing one-third of the work. Citizens should also be aware that time is short for various reasons. In the first place, because we don't know how long it will be before the arrival of a new pandemic, compounding the consequences of COVID-19, but also because the progression of climate change will limit the global planting capacity for those trees. With the current climate, it is estimated that there is a potential for 4.4 billion hectares of tree cover – that is, there is still room for planting 0.9 billion hectares. Climate change will alter this capacity, and estimates show that the climate in 2050 will be able to support 223 million fewer hectares, with the most fundamental losses occurring in the tropics (Bastin et al., 2019).

Thus, I would invite the citizens to engage in activism in the streets, on social media, in the exercise of their professions, and in their exercise of the right vote, in demanding the urgent implementation of definitive anti-pollution measures with irreversible low emission

18 https://epha.org/coronavirus-threat-greater-for-polluted-cities/
19 https://epha.org/wp-content/uploads/2018/07/Clean-air-briefing.pdf

zones, and in demanding that these areas not only limit circulation, but that they also incorporate tree planting measures, in demanding that these measures be put in place urgently, and in demanding an ambitious policy of increasing green spaces in the city, over the long term. It is also important that the response to this demand take place over the long term. since the cities that have been most successful and ambitious in implementing these measures have shown determination in the implementation of various phases. San Francisco, for example, has been following a progressive policy. It began with plans, approved in 2005, which transferred the maintenance of the city's trees, then in private hands, to the public administration, which involves caring for an estimated 105,000 trees throughout their useful lives and planting 50,000 new trees through 2035. In addition, the planting of specific species on private property has also been encouraged, and under the third phase, effective as of January 1, 2017, roofs that include solar panels, green roofs, or a combination of the two are now mandatory in new constructions.

A Forested, yet Dense City with Public Transportation

No doubt the first time that someone imagined that the city and the country could be compatible, and that it would make sense and be desirable to mix them in a hybrid urban model, was in 1890. That was when Ebenezer Howard wrote *To-morrow: A Peaceful Path to Real Reform,* which was published in 1898 and significantly reformulated and published again in 1902 under the title *Garden Cities of To-morrow.* The book was written at a time when a significant part of the English population was migrating from the countryside to the city. London gained 1.25 million inhabitants between 1841 and 1911, a large number of whom were women who went to work in urban houses as domestic servants (Zimmerman and Bauer, 2002), and for whom this emigration mainly meant leaving behind the clean air of the countryside and being subjected to industrial environments with enormous public health deficiencies. It is estimated that in the same period 4.5 million rural inhabitants moved to live in mainly industrial urban destinations, although agriculture only lost 0.75 million workers (Zimmerman and Bauer, 2002). Howard, inspired by reformist thinking, fundamentally sought to provide a good life for the city-dwellers: "Its object is, in short, to raise the standard of health and comfort of all true workers of whatever grade – the means by which these objects are to be achieved being a healthy, natural and economic combination of town and country life," (Howard, 2001: 51). As seen in this declaration of intent, what is still interesting about Howard's approach is that he focused urban planning efforts on comprehensive personal and group development, in which health, economy, productivity, socialization and natural preservation were all part of the goals in a balanced way. It is well known how he illustrated the objectives his city pursued, verbally and graphically, as the balance of three magnets. The "country" magnet offered advantages such as fresh air, low rents, abundance of water and sunshine, and access to meadows and forests, but it also had its disadvantages, such as unemployment or a lack of amusement. The "town" magnet provided social opportunities, places of amusement, chances of employment, and palatial edifices, but forced people to suffer the inconveniences of distance from work, chances of unemployment, slums, excessive hours, and foul air. The "countryside-city" magnet combined the advantages of both: access to employment and entertainment as well as pure air, sun, clean water and the beauty of nature. In reading Howard's book, we see that productive activities did not yet enjoy the predominance they subsequently obtained.

Howard proposed building new garden cities for a fixed population of 30,000, which would be self-sufficient and surrounded by an agricultural belt where no construction would be allowed. The cities would be managed by cooperative public corporations in which all the inhabitants would participate. The program for the self-sufficiency of cities not only included the agricultural belt and the means of production (factories and offices), but also the leisure facilities necessary to entertain the population.

Howard had the opportunity to participate in the design and construction of two garden cities, Letchworth and Welwyn Garden, which greatly influenced the development of suburban areas in the UK and the rest of Europe, and the world. In later years, as sustainability criteria have become relevant, garden cities and the type of suburban areas generated by their repetition have been deemed highly unsustainable due to two fundamental criteria: their low density and their dependence on private vehicles. Letchworth covers an area of 2,012 hectares and has about 33,000 inhabitants. That means it has a density of about five dwellings per hectare.

Different authors have established that a density of 60 dwellings per hectare is the minimum so that public transport can be effective, for example, and so that there can be a desirable mix of uses and a certain anonymity (López de Lucio, 2007). In my doctoral dissertation,[20] I wrote at length about the paradox generated by that assessment. The image that has historically been associated with sustainable development is a green one: the garden city in urban planning; and buildings with green roofs or even green façades in architecture. These "visual" intuitions can lead to considerable errors when it comes to impact assessment. In terms of public transport use, Manhattan is one of the most efficient urban areas in the United States, but its visual aspect is far from what we intuitively associate with sustainable development.

When we introduce the pollution variable into this difficult equation, we come up against a double paradox: the presence of greenery can be misleading in determining the sustainability of an urban area.

20 http://oa.upm.es/42328/1/IZASKUN_CHINCHILLA_MORENO.pdf

Where the pursuit of green spaces leads to lower density and greater dependence on private vehicles, those urban areas will deviate from acceptable sustainability standards. Here is the first paradox: "green" does not mean "good" (in terms of sustainability). On the other hand, in a second look at the real impact of pollution on health and the effectiveness of planting trees in the fight against the climate emergency, "green" would mean "strictly necessary".

We might say that, in certain parts of the planet, the climate emergency can challenge the principles of sustainability derived from the Brundtland report. The best urban planning should strike a balance, for example, in terms of densities, between a functional density that makes public transport viable and a density of greenery associated with the climate response and pollution.

In the architecture studio I direct, we have made several attempts to combine these parameters. At the end of 2003, I had the privilege of winning one of the EUROPAN prizes in Santiago de Compostela. EUROPAN is a biennial competition for urban projects designed by architects under 40 years of age from all over Europe. It has been held since 1989. It is one of the most prestigious architecture awards for emerging architects, and one of the few chances a fledging studio has of getting a commission on an urban scale. In my case, having won the award did not mean that the project was carried out, but it served to cement the principles of what we might call a *forest city*, which aimed to overcome some of the problems of the garden city.

The proposal foresaw building the city based on units covering one square hectare: each unit was a 100 x 100 meter square. Between 20% and 30% was allocated to construction, while the remaining free space was divided into two areas (each occupying between 30% and 40% of the remaining square footage), the city area and the forested area. The city area included an urbanized zone, respecting the natural runoff of the land where circulation could coexist flexibly with other occupations of open space (e.g., open-air cinema, sports). In the forested areas, the proposal incorporated a dense and continuous tree plantation. The circulation across both areas was arranged diagonally, reducing by 65% the length and occupation of roads, compared to a configuration situating the circulation areas along the perimeter. At the entrance to each unit, citizens could choose whether to cycle or walk through the forest area or the city area, whereas circulation in private vehicles was limited to the city area.

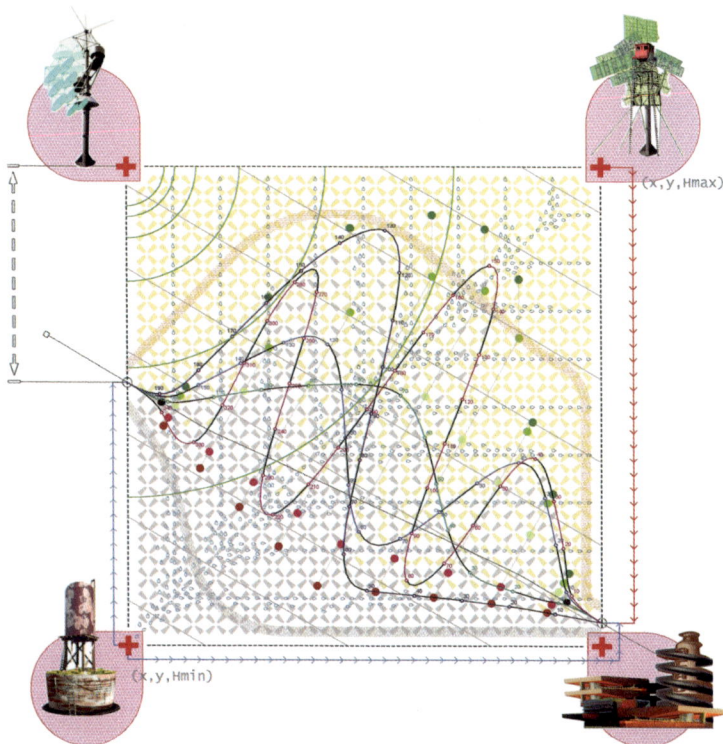

(x,y,Hmax)

(x,y,Hmin)

Europan Santiago. Diagram of basic urban units.
©Izaskun Chinchilla Architects.

This proposal sought to recover some of the attractions that Ebenezer Howard proposed for the garden city, eliminating the two major problems that, subsequently, have made the garden city an unsustainable development model: low density and dependence on the private vehicle. In our design for the A Pulleira estate, we exceeded the density of 60 dwellings per hectare, while at the same time eight hectares of the 30 occupied by the development were allocated to dense tree planting. This was possible, in part, because the grid of diagonal roads allowed for a 65% reduction in occupancy with respect to the standard of urban planning using a square grid, taking advantage of that space for dense tree planting.

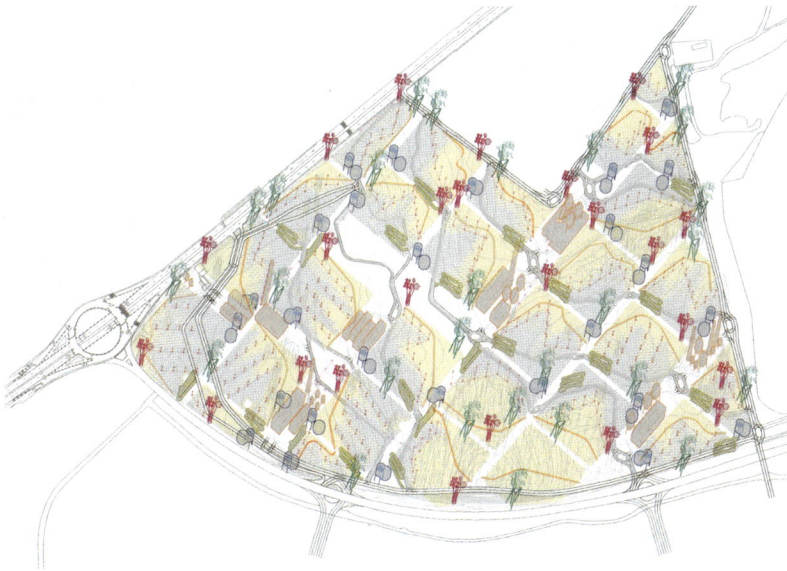

Europan Santiago. Site plan.
©Izaskun Chinchilla Architects.

unidades metros.
escala 1 / 800.

Europan Santiago. Site plan, detail.
©Izaskun Chinchilla Architects.

But, moreover, the project aims to empower pedestrians. In many cities around the world – think of Los Angeles, for example, or most Latin American capitals, having a private car means being able to get where you want to go. Your possibilities as a pedestrian are severely limited, not just by distances, but above all by the lack of urban continuity. While the space for vehicles is conceived as a continuum of streets, highways, avenues and boulevards, pedestrians constantly encounter impassable barriers. The caring city, in this sense, must be structured around a continuous pedestrian fabric, no doubt also suitable for bikes and other low-impact vehicles, but which reserves the best connectivity for pedestrians and guarantees universal accessibility, while also inheriting the continuous pedestrian condition of traditional Mediterranean cities.

This is also one of the points to be re-imagined from the garden city model, which has often treated sidewalks as residual spaces that are either not completely continuous or given priority, or which are so deserted, because of very low density, that they are not safe. The neuroscientist and author of *In Praise of Walking*, Shane O'Mara (2019), goes further by taking "activist" attempting not to stop to wait for cars to pass, interrupting traffic when necessary, since he considers that pedestrians, as a social group, should not "have to ask permission to cross the street". A city that follows his precepts should be organized around a continuous flow of pedestrian connectivity, which should be considered a priority, reserving the gaps in the natural flow of pedestrians for the passage of vehicles. In this way, the city would begin to generate an active care of its citizens.

Another important aspect of the caring city – with the aim not only of reducing pollution, but also generating active care for citizens – is to recover some of the features of the garden city that Howard envisioned but that were never implemented. I am referring, specifically, to the agricultural belt that was to designed surround the garden city and ensure it could be self-sufficient.

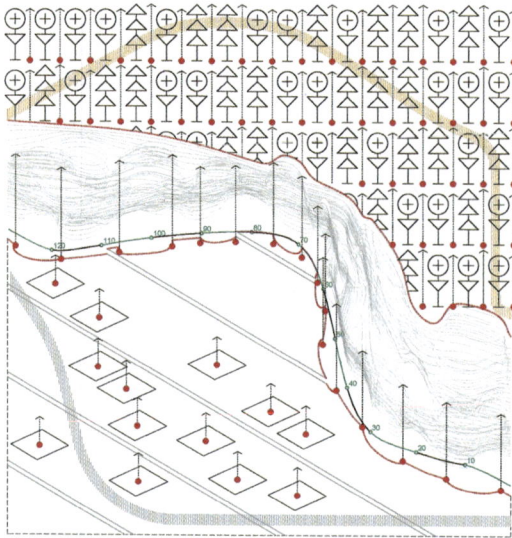

Espartalia Housing Development. Site plan detail, building b4.
©Izaskun Chinchilla Architects.

The combination of the forest city and urban developments' absorption of the agricultural footprint would be an excellent policy to support a more quantitative and territorial understanding of sustainability, if you will. The problem with including this agricultural footprint is that it would further decrease population density. In the studio we developed a project for the Espartalia housing development, in Hellín (Albacete), in which we tried to achieve a more rural character absorbing the agricultural footprint, including water consumption, in the urban development, while preventing the drop in density from condemning the development to being dependent on private vehicles. To that effect, the construction was planned around compact cores, with a density of more than 70 dwellings per hectare, which held collective housing, shops and facilities, and which was connected by roads. Around those dense cores, there is a range of lower density units (35 dwellings/ha), of semi-detached houses, which can be accessed by their owners only from the denser cores. Concentrically there is a range of even lower density units, of free-standing single-family homes to which only emergency access is available, and whose energy management is considered off-the-grid (Chinchilla, 2007).

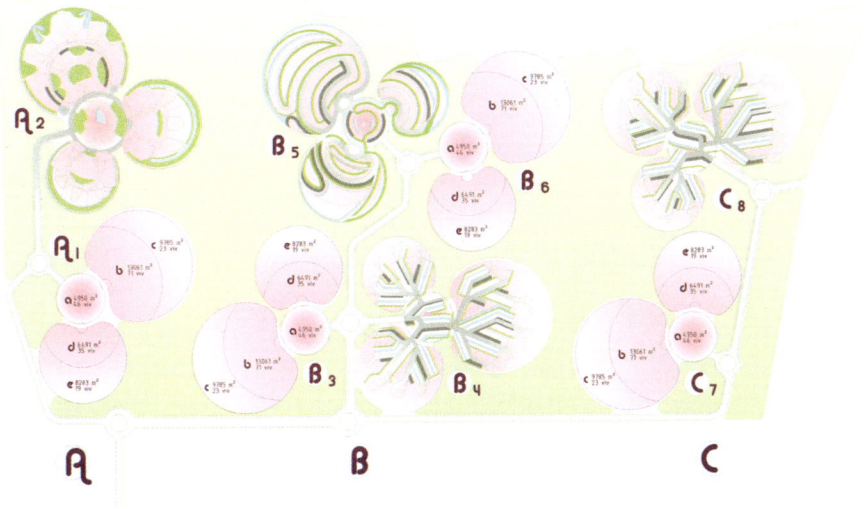

Espartalia Housing Development. Site plan.
©Izaskun Chinchilla Architects.

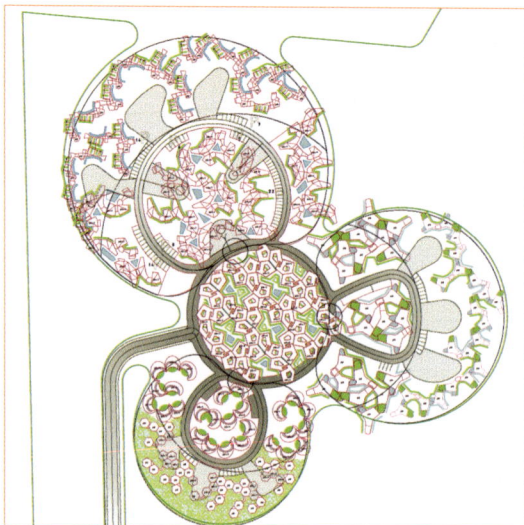

Espartalia Housing Development. Site plan detail, building a2.and b4. ©Izaskun Chinchilla Architects.

The caring city, therefore, must reassess the reduction of pollution and the redensification of green spaces as an urgent priority. In the existing urban areas, or in areas where limited alterations can be carried out, it will be necessary to opt for enabling low-emission areas, reducing the presence of vehicles, and implementing an active policy of planting trees in them. In urban expanses, new cities or intensive urban reforms, a dynamic control of density should be adopted to restructure the importance of pedestrian connectivity, making it into the backbone of the urban order and making it compatible with dense tree planting and with the reabsorption, if only partial, of the agricultural footprint.

Espartalia Housing Development. Collage.
©Izaskun Chinchilla Architects.

Espartalia Housing Development. Render aerial view.
©Izaskun Chinchilla Architects.

CHAPTER 6 BENCHES YOU CAN'T LIE DOWN ON VERSUS THE HOME WITHOUT A HOUSE

Examples of Hostile Architecture

We have gotten used to coexisting, for example in airports, with design inventions aimed at preventing rest. One good example of this are benches with armrests installed intermittently along their lengths to prevent users from lying down. Now it seems that, in some cities, these impediments to rest are becoming so widespread that they have been given the generic title of "hostile architecture", which has its own entry on Wikipedia and has been criticized by any number of progressive newspapers around the world.[21]

Hostile architecture relies on different types of devices. One important category are the aforementioned benches that prevent anyone from lying down on them. They come in several types: the kind with armrests interspersed along their length; the kind that are angled so that you can lean up against them but you can't actually sit

---

21. https://www.nytimes.com/2019/11/08/nyregion/hostile-architecture-nyc.html, https://www.publico.es/tremending/2019/12/29/la-vuelta-al-mundo-de-la-ar- quitectura-hostil-para-personas-sin-techo/

on them; benches made from metal tubes which, again, one can lean against but can't sit comfortably on, and lying down is, of course, impossible; and short benches, which serve the same purpose.

Another of the elements most commonly seen in hostile architecture are sharp elements. They are installed anywhere that might accommodate a human body lying down, or sometimes even sitting down, especially if the area offers protection against the wind or inclement weather. These sharp elements have become popular on low ledges and fences, in areas under bridges or at the entrances to ATM machines, among other places. Similar elements are also beginning to be used on railings and other kinds of hard and prominent surfaces found in parks and squares to obstruct certain sports and urban leisure, especially parkour and skateboarding.

Hostile architecture is more present in privately owned public spaces or "POPS". Here, more often than not, we also find the most traditional and least innovative mechanism of this type of architecture: the fence. The historical evolution of these spaces shows that there are different ways of managing the ownership of public space, and citizens' rights in it, and that these forms of management are broadly influenced by the prevailing political ideology. Although the nuances in the management of public space are broad, we're dealing with, on the one hand, a strong historical current that has defended that public spaces should be public property and, on the other, tendencies and ideologies that defend different degrees of private participation in places in the city subject to collective access. Different cities and countries around the world have recently aligned themselves with these two trends, applying them with nuances in keeping with different political, ethical, historical and philosophical criteria, which on many occasions – especially in recent times – have not been subjected to public debate or consulted with citizens ahead of time (Kayden, 2000).

It is worth offering a brief historical overview and remembering that the transformation of privately owned open urban spaces into publicly owned property has been an ongoing practice in recent decades and for centuries in many European cities. One of many possible examples are the community gardens present in many squares around London. When they were first introduced in the early 17th century, they were conceived as fenced gardens, at the center of a square, surrounded by residential buildings and which were accessible, privately, to the owners of the dwellings around them. Thus, these precious green spaces were only accessible to those who owned one of the homes that opened onto the square (Lawrence, 1993). The owners would have a key to the gate and could use the garden in keeping with certain rules.

The evolution of democratic ideals regarding public space meant that most of these squares were converted into public parks over the course of the 20th century. This can be seen as a general trend not only in London, but throughout Europe. It has been the case in Bedford, Notting Hill and Bloomsbury in London, along with other cities in the UK such as Edinburgh, Bath, Bristol and Leeds. But it has also happened in Paris (Place des Vosges, Square des Épinettes, Place Royal), Dublin (Merrion Square, Fitzwilliam Square, Mountjoy Square, St Stephen's Green, Parnell Square) and Brussels (Square de Meeûs, Square Orban). In the transition from the 17th to the 20th century, European countries democratized open spaces in the city, turning former royal properties into public parks (Ives, Clark, Walter, 2018) or disentailing properties belonging to the Church. In general, most countries have undertaken a certain transformation of properties associated with pre-democratic regimes and have turned them into public spaces, with many of these processes culminating in the 20th century. These transformations are the result of extensive political and social debates about the rights to city of the aristocracy, the Church, the religious orders and other instances of mortmain, and how those rights should be balanced with those of the bulk of the population.

But, since 1961, as a result of the new regulations called the New York Zoning Resolution, legal incentives began to be offered in the city, such as expanding floor area ratios for buildings with spaces open to the public on the street level (Kayden, 2000), promoting a new generation of POPS that continues to this day, fundamentally in the United States, Asia and Latin America, since similar regulations are widespread in those areas. Today, cities like San Francisco, Boston, Detroit, Santiago de Chile, Hong Kong, Tokyo or São Paulo all have them. Numerous POPS have also emerged in Europe in recent decades, initially associated with shopping centers that set up "squares" or galleries with cafes or outdoor spaces. They have also been frequent in residential areas developed through the open block typology and, lately, they have flourished, offering very diverse management formulas, in cities like London.[22] It seems like, after determining that certain rights over the city were unacceptable for the structures inherited from old regimes, a parallel movement, emerging slightly later, deemed that some of those same privileges were admissible, given certain exchanges, for private companies and consortiums.

There are, of course, discrepancies between these two tendencies when it comes to the conception of ownership and the management of public space. On the one hand, there is a more pragmatic vision that points to the advantages of POPS as places that can provide better facilities and maintenance at lower public cost and which, with adequate efforts towards placemaking, can emulate the social role of traditional public spaces and provide a fully urban experience (Carmona, 2014) where there is no noticeable empirical evidence

22 https://en.wikipedia.org/wiki/List_of_privately_owned_public_spaces_in_London

of segregation, at least in some of the geographic areas in which monitoring has taken place (Langstraat and Van Melik, 2013).

But there are still a significant number of architects and urban planners who think that private ownership destroys the true meaning of public space (Mitchell, 2017), aligning with the logic put forth by Habermas, according to which the public sphere is conceptualized as the series of institutions and activities that mediate between the State and society. In this public sphere, society is organized and finds its representation, and its public character is fundamental because any form of social organization must be provided with equal access to the structures of power (Habermas, 1999).

The fact that hostile architecture is more abundant in POPS, and especially in places where POPS are more common and have existed for a longer period of time, reveals that many people's reticence to them may have considerable relevance. Hostile architecture is fundamentally directed against a specific and especially vulnerable segment of society: homeless people. Also, although to a lesser extent, it tries to hinder the activities of other groups, such as those who practice certain urban sports or those who eat or drink alcohol in the city or even those who spend a lot of time sitting down and occupying the same space, among others.

At least 160 cities in the United States, including New York, Los Angeles and Chicago, prohibit camping, sitting or lying down in public spaces or outdoors, according to the 2016 National Law Center on Homelessness and Poverty Report. The public investments directed at criminalizing homeless people are greater than what is allocated toward preventing and addressing the problems they suffer. The cost of arresting a homeless person, for example, in Colorado in 2014, was estimated to be $645.17. That is how much it cost to transport a homeless person to the police station, keep them there for one night, and release them the next morning. The total spending for 2014 corresponding to this type of arrest amounted to $742,790.18. Redirecting this spending toward public housing would mean being able to provide at least 20 homes per year.

The regulations against the homeless are not effective in improving the problems of this group of people or in preserving other groups from any tangible harm. In most cases, this is because the people writing the regulations on the public space consider certain lifestyles to be better or more desirable than others, tending toward a form of organization of the city that has been called "teleocracy" because its implicit objective is the promotion of a hegemonic way of life (Alexander, Mazza and Moroni, 2012). The regulations on the consumption of alcohol, the consumption of food, praying in public, the kind language that can be used, the iconography of storefronts, the expression of different cultural aspects, the collection of signatures, prostitution or camping that exist in public spaces in many parts of the world hardly ever prevent material or personal damage or loss; what they do is promote a lifestyle.

A good balance between the practical aspects and the philosophical aspects of public space is struck by those who argue that regulations on public space should aim to prevent only those actions that cause tangible harm to third parties, while avoiding imposing a moral criterion regarding what kinds of lifestyles are desirable. In this sense, some defend that public spaces should be subject to absolutely minimal restrictions, seeking out the optimum expression of maximum tolerance and trusting that forms of coexistence can be achieved through dialogue, in a form of administration that has been called "monocracy" (Alexander, Mazza and Moroni, 2012), in opposition to the aforementioned teleocracy.

From the point of view of citizens, this is a fundamental claim that can shed further light on the recent COVID-19 crisis and help us understand its full magnitude. Let's look at an example: in many public spaces we have accepted that fountains will be emptied so that no one can bathe in them. Are we not denying a fundamental right in this, all the more in the recent pandemic scenario? This results in a greater difficulty for subsistence among the urban population, and it affects biodiversity. With this gesture, we make it impossible for children, the elderly, and people with disabilities to cool down quickly and free of charge, or to assert their rights and demand measures to ensure hygienic conditions. When we allow a teleocratic administration of public space, we are sometimes allowing a violation of many citizens' fundamental rights, along with countless collateral effects.

Have we finally understood, as a society affected by COVID-19, that everyone's health is interrelated, both among citizens and with the environment and the natural surroundings? Citizens need to demand positive action from municipal governments to guarantee universal access to rest and hygiene in public spaces, and they should demand that, before privatizing the places we share, measures should be imposed to guarantee that the companies and consortiums that currently contribute to their management, and even own them, have access to those rights.

The Home without a House Project (Hogar sin casa)

Around 2006, we presented a project to several city councils in Murcia that intended to contribute to the preservation of the Huerta de Murcia (Abellán and Chinchilla, 2010).

The city of Murcia sits in a geographical enclave called the Huerta de Murcia, which has undergone a transformation over the last 50 years, – in an unregulated and unplanned process in many cases – that has led to the formation of a very complex space in terms of urban planning. On the one hand, it is articulated as a city with multiple cores, with a central nucleus (the city proper), and about 60 peripheral nuclei (called districts). On the other hand, the agrarian continuum that once supported this structure, equipped (beginning in the 12th century under Islamic influence) with an extensive network of irrigation ditches and rural roads, has been subject to spontaneous construction, without planning, which has resulted in the practical disappearance (in some cases) of the agrarian environment in favor of a peri-urban territory, with scant urban quality (Temes Cordovez et al., 2018).

The Huerta is under enormous pressure, because it is used as a space for leisure and urban expansion for the city of Murcia. The most aggressive aspect of this pressure are the second homes that have built, in many cases illegally, at an increasingly rapid rate leading up to 2007: whereas through the end of the 1990s the usual rate of growth in the number of houses was 5% per decade, from 1991 to 2001 the increase was 18%, and between 2001 and 2005 alone it was 24.89%.[23] Despite the slowdown brought about by the economic crisis, this rapid rise has created a serious environmental challenge due to the impact of the uncontrolled shift in land use, the emissions associated with construction, the increase in water consumption, the increase in private vehicles, and, therefore, pollution and other associated phenomena (Martí Ciriquián and Moreno Vicente, 2014).

We called our project "Home without a House". The main proposal was to allow the use of the Huerta as an educational and recreational

23 The 1991 housing census for the Region of Murcia showed a total of 482,160. Ten years later, in the 2001 census, that figure was 571,604, representing an increase of 89,444; the rise over that 10-year period amounted to 18%. Most extraordinarily, in the last five years (for which information is available), from 2001 to 2005, 142,320 new housing permits were issued, many more than the total for the entire preceding decade. That represents an increase of 24.89% over the previous census figure – i.e., an annual average cumulative increase of close to 5% per year. (Serrano and Garcia, 2007).

space while avoiding the construction of holiday homes and instead offering, in a public and shared regime, a program of activities similar to those engaged in on a usual weekend by the owners of second residences. The development of the project included a series of public infrastructures that, if reviewed and refined today, could provide new opportunities for the conservation of the surrounding environment.

The first of these infrastructures is a series of parking spaces, which would be located in the capital of Murcia and at controlled points in the Huerta so that access would take place using a shared electric vehicle. The parking spaces would be covered with organic material such as esparto grass, hemp, jute or pita, derived from grassy or shrubby plants that are common in the area due to the dry climate. This would help boost the activity of the network of local artisans who work with these materials, offering at the same time a biodegradable construction that minimizes impact not only in the construction

Home without a House. Elevation of the outdoor rooms.
©Izaskun Chinchilla Architects.

Home without a House. Axonometric drawing, cart in the shade.
©Izaskun Chinchilla Architects.

but also in the subsequent demolition and recycling. The parking spaces, strategically located in the Huerta to control the density of visitors, would be equipped with solar panels. The shared electric vehicle could be outfitted with specific equipment, for example, a refrigerator, so that the cars could be used for storage. The vehicle GPS would contain specific podcasts on the history of the Huerta, leisure offers and environmental prevention campaigns.

From these parking spaces, located on the perimeter of the Huerta, all trips would take place using public bicycles equipped with a navigator, which can be picked up in the aforementioned parking spaces. These bicycles with a browser would suggest itineraries and leisure activities, updated in real time, avoiding overcrowding in the different recreational areas and allowing for the control of a maximum number of visitors and users.

Home without a House. Axonometric drawing, cart in the shade.
©Izaskun Chinchilla Architects.

One of the proposed activities involved choosing a traditional recipe, which could be entered in the bike navigator; it would offer an itinerary through the Huerta to obtain the ingredients, to be purchased directly from the producers in the area. The browser would show the name, surname, address and contact information for the producers facilitating the establishment of commercial relationships with the visitors – normally inhabitants of urban areas. The recipe book from Murcia, rich and extensive, contains, of course, many recipes based on the consumption of products from the garden. They include *zarangollo*, *pisto de la vega media*, and *mojete*. Some ingredients might be kept in the cars or imported to the Huerta from nearby regions, such as rice from Calasparra, and it would visitors to discover the extensive regional cuisine, enriched with products from the Huerta.

Home without a House. Axonometric drawing, Accessories for shopping with a backpack. ©Izaskun Chinchilla Architects.

One of the most important infrastructures in the Home without a House project was the shared kitchens. They consisted of lightweight furniture, protected from the elements by awnings, and offered a cooking area and a tasting area. The furniture in the cooking area consisted essentially of three strips. A top strip for solar panels and water containers, an intermediate strip for food storage and a countertop for preparing it. The combination of the three strips forms a self-sufficient kitchen in energetic terms, equipped with passive systems to preserve the food, and the necessary tools and equipment for the preparation of local recipes. The use of the kitchen invited us to better understand the local ecosystem, understand how the climate favored the collection of spices in certain seasons, and to rediscover vernacular traditions, such as the use of salting, pickling or garlic, which historically made it possible to enjoy similar meals with less energy dependency.

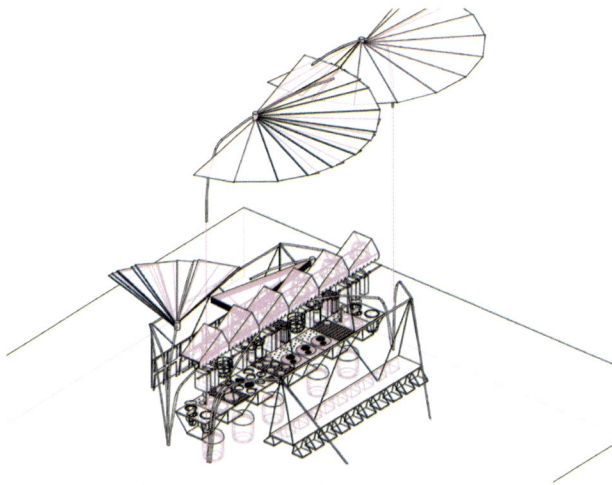

Home without a House. Axonometric drawing. Bulk kitchen with a table for 20 people. ©Izaskun Chinchilla Architects.

In addition to the kitchens, there were games using water coming from, and recirculated to, the irrigation ditches using waterwheels, preferential areas set up for napping. There was even a proposal for a beer pit. For more sheltered rest areas, hanging esparto grass structures were set up to offer shade and good ventilation.

This intervention is not considered a solution to the possible problems of the Huerta. These problems, like almost all the lasting problems in the city, originate and develop under the influence of multiple factors, and no isolated action can "solve" them. What we can achieve with tactically well-developed projects is to alter the conditions under which the links and connections between the different actors and actants can generate new opportunities that will give rise to slightly different results in the chains of action, and which can potentially generate beneficial effects (Berry, 1981: Chapter 9). Thus, it is important not to posit this project as a solution, but rather as a modification to the "rules of the game". And although I think one of the most important lessons that students of architecture and urban planning should learn is that environmental and urban problems don't have a single solution, much less an easy one, it is also important to transmit a certain confidence that small actions can have beneficial and restorative consequences. Various researchers who have studied property rights as they pertain to natural resources have highlighted the need to compensate for exclusions (Sikor, He, Lestrelin, 2020). This perspective, often of a bottom-up nature, encompasses a wide range of actors and agents at the local, regional, national and international levels, and it proposes the recognition of new rights – specifically, the provision of indirect benefits and authority rights, broadening the perspective of governance beyond a dualistic view of property (public or private).

The House without a Home project can compensate for the exclusion that only the owners of a plot or a home can enjoy the leisure and education benefits offered by the Huerta. It can also compensate for the laxity of urban planning in recent decades, which has been lenient toward the irregular construction of second homes, providing municipal representatives with rights of authority over the occupancy that can be permitted in different places. Lastly, Home without a House made it possible to distribute indirect benefits among different local agents: espadrille craftspeople or vegetable farmers who can sell their products to end users, among others. Once again, better management of environmental problems refers to greater complexity in governance that goes beyond the usual "black boxes"[24] such as the simplified concepts of property, public ownership or the State.

24 Just as Latour points out that science "blackboxes" the basic physical principles driving the machines that surround us, (Latour, 2001), I assume in this text that urban planning law turns larger concepts such as "property" or "the State" into black boxes – into categories without internal complexity.

In the exploitation and management of many natural resources, it is common for citizens to remain excluded from the exercise of authority rights (for example, Ribot et al., 2006) and for the rights of local owners to be restricted to secondary benefits (for example, Edmunds and Wollenberg, 2003). In these contexts, the distribution of indirect benefits, such as those we have mentioned in the case of the Huerta, can change in the medium and long term and reinforce, from the bottom up, the positions of agents who have been historically excluded.

A similar vision could be applied to the very difficult problem of homelessness in the city. In January 2016, Senator Carol Liu introduced a proposal to protect homeless people's rights to sleep or rest in public spaces in California. The proposition called SB 876 would decriminalize the behavior, limiting the capabilities of local authorities and regulations to treat the fact of sleeping on the street as a criminal act and making it illegal to destroy, requisition or move homeless people's property without their permission. Obtaining this right does not solve the problems of homeless people in Los Angeles, for example, where the homeless crisis has been the object of extensive studies and proposals, such as the "Homeless Strategy", a 240-page document that studies everything from public housing policies to the operation of shelters, with limited results. But for highly skilled agents, it would have an immense effect.[25] As we mentioned previously, SB 876 would compensate for a historical exclusion by granting very indirect benefits – the right to rest in public space and to store property there – and would severely alter the rules.

Combining SB 876 with a monocratic regulation of public space, which would be permissive and inclusive of all lifestyles, would

25 Eric Ares, social worker and coordinator of the Los Angeles Community Action Network.

return the rights of authority to the citizens themselves. The homeless would probably continue to experience exclusion, but they would be surrounded by more tolerant cities and communities.

This same perspective of compensation for exclusions through the distribution of indirect benefits and rights of authority can be applied to POPS. Without resorting to a simplifying duality in which public ownership is good and private ownership is undesirable, we are obliged to assume that, by definition, POPS imply exclusion: they entail a reduction in the rights of citizens who do not own the space, and, very often, a reduction in the rights of citizens who are not potential clients of the businesses that operate there. It is therefore necessary to compensate for this exclusion by granting indirect rights and authority rights. From the point of view of building the caring city, these actions must be aimed at protecting rest and health. Those who reside in an area of terraces and hotel services should have an administrative right that ensures the enactment of schedules compatible with rest. The people who are not customers of the businesses should be granted indirect rights: to be able drink clean water for free, to be able to go to the bathroom, to be able to bathe, to rest, to be protected from the elements, to have access to clean air and safe streets. Perhaps, in the times before the COVID-19 crisis, it might have seemed that these were excessive rights, but given today's perspective, not only is it fair for those who exploit a public space for commercial purposes to possess certain rights and obligations, but, fundamentally, we have seen that only civil liability with the State and a strict commitment to the repeal of historic exclusions can generate a city where economic activity as we know it continues to be viable.

CHAPTER 7 HARD SURFACES VERSUS A LANDSCAPE IN STRIPS

The Culture of Hard Surfaces

In urban design, the term *plazas duras*, or squares paved with hard surfaces, is used to refer to solutions for the urbanization of public spaces that consist of an extensive paved surface, normally granite or concrete, with hardly any vegetation and, more often than not, scant street furniture.

The quintessential example around which this model was built was the Plaça dels Països Catalans, the work of the architects Albert Viaplana and Helio Piñón, with collaboration from Enric Miralles, which became a symbol of the new urbanism that put the Catalan capital on the international map in the 1980s. It won the FAD Award for Architecture in 1984, and in 2019 it was designated by the Barcelona City Council as a cultural heritage site that deserves special protection. The square covers an area of more than two hectares, although it does not have any landscaping – partly because it was built above an immense railway yard. Its original design incorporates two canopies: a central, taller one, which offers scant protection from the elements due to its thin transparent roof; and another with a wavy profile, lower in height and crossing the square in a straight line, which, although it is outfitted with some furniture (fewer than a dozen benches with built-in tables), seems intended only to protect passengers heading toward the station entrance. Despite the fact that the square serves as the entrance to the Estació de Sants, which has received more than 10,000 passengers a day for decades, there was a limited provision of benches in the original design. This was later complemented by another 30 that formed a winding line, entirely unprotected from the sun or the rain, and which, strangely enough, were installed around the periphery of the square, very close to the busiest surrounding street, Carrer de Viriat.

It is worth noting the historical, political and economic circumstances that surrounded the design of this paved square in order to understand the virtues it pursued. In 1979, in the context of burgeoning democracy, the PSUC, the Socialist party, came to power in the Barcelona City Council. The 1980s in Barcelona were characterized by a scarcity of resources, by the beginning of the city's Olympic aspirations, which ended up coming true in 1992, and by a powerful grassroots movement that was often at odds with the local administration. In 1980, the architect Oriol Bohigas joined the Planning Department. His vision of how to revitalize Barcelona consisted of a strong commitment to the construction of small public spaces in various different neighborhoods across the city. He closed the Plaça Reial to traffic, tore down a city block in El Raval and reinforced the public squares in Sants and Gràcia. This scattered use of the department budget – compared with other municipal management models that opted for a new Master Plan, like Madrid, or for concentrating investment around paradigmatic streets and unique elements – also meant that the allocation for each of the interventions was limited.

In addition to these political and economic conditions, the *plaza dura* is part of a conception that was also fueled by major contributions from Ignasi de Solà-Morales. His writings offer us a better understanding of the design intent implicit in these types of solutions. In the chapter "Place: Permanence or Production", from his book *Differences: Topographies of Contemporary Architecture* (1995), he contrasts a static and sacred concept of place with the idea of flow, dynamism, a sequence of events, and the convergence of energies on the site. Furthermore, Solà-Morales argued that what he called *terrains vagues*, semi-abandoned spaces without a functional definition, were the true essence of urbanity; they provided an anonymous freedom, which citizens could exercise uninhibited by the capitalist determination of other spaces in the city, which dictated specific actions for each place and imposed consumption.

The main criticisms of the so-called "Barcelona model", consolidated and articulated in a large part by Oriol Bohigas, (he is credited with having had as much decision-making power as Haussmann in Paris or Otto Wagner in Vienna)[26] can also be applied to the paved square. Josep Maria Montaner (2013) highlights the lack of dialogue with neighborhood associations, the lack of protection and appreciation for historical heritage (for example, four warehouses designed by Elies Rogent, considered essential to the birth of Modernism, were demolished to build the Rambla Litoral, and Bohigas himself said on several occasions that the best fate for the Sagrada Família would be as a commuter train stopover), and the failure to incorporate criteria of sustainability. From today's perspective, further criticisms could be added to this list, such as the absence of a gender perspective or the lack of a contribution to a vision of placemaking which incorporates a real observation, assimilation, and integration of the needs and desires of the users of the spaces.

26 "For a while, he was the architect with the most decision-making power in the world, after Haussmann in Paris and Otto Wagner in Vienna," says his colleague and friend, the architect Oscar Tusquets, at https://www.elperiodlco.com/es/cuaderno/20161220/oriol-bohigas-el-cerebro-del-modelo-barcelona-4763729

In fact, in delving into what has been called "the disconnect between architects and society", the paved square and the example of the Plaça dels Països Catalans could serve as incredibly valuable case studies. In 2017, José Mansilla, urban anthropologist and member of the Observatori d'Antropologia del Conflicte Urbà (OACU),[27] undertook a study as part of his course "Introduction to the Sociology and Psychology of Tourism", through a brief exercise in participant observation involving users. Most of the participants in the study did not think of the site as a square; they perceived it as an ugly, dirty space they had to cross through but with little use of its own. When asked what elements they would add to the square, the answers suggested giving the scenery a little more color, green areas to provide cleaner air for pedestrians, benches and spaces for collective rest, avoiding isolated installations that obstruct conversation and, finally, the incorporation of children's play areas, a dog run, and a designated area exclusively for skateboarders. In relation to the broader context, the participants called for traffic calming, cutting back on the presence of vehicles in general and connecting the area with the nearby Avinguda de Roma.

Two years after this study took place, the square was listed by experts as a cultural heritage site and, therefore, must be maintained in a state as close to the original as possible. It is one of the many examples of the divergences between experts' opinions and residents' desires. Where some see an example of architectural heritage that should be preserved for posterity, others do not recognize it as a square or even a minimally comfortable space.

All of the above has not prevented the paved square from remaining a highly successful model, which continues to be replicated in many urban sites above train tracks that have not been urbanized, and where landscaping would have been entirely possible. In Madrid

27 http://www.ub.edu/grecs/2013/04/observatori-antropologia-del-conflicte-urba-oacu-2/

alone, the squares Callao, Ópera, Puerta del Sol, Tirso de Molina, Lavapiés, Santo Domingo, Pedro Zerolo, Chueca or Los Cubos have all followed this model. Citizen indignation has been widespread, with marked vehemence in places like Seville. In 2016, the journalist Carlos Colón wrote in the *Diario de Sevilla*: "The paved Plaza de Arms and Plaza de Santa Justa were designed to screw over the city's residents, to disorient them, scorch them and reduce them to insects, in a gesture worthy of Kafka, as they cross through a desolate and blazing helplessness."

While paved squares have already earned their fair share of enemies, we can only hope that climate change will definitively do away with their prestige among teams of municipal architects and experts. Squares that are paved with hard surfaces contribute extraordinarily to the well-known "heat island" effect, the urban phenomenon whereby the temperatures in cities are consistently higher throughout the year compared to rural areas within a radius of 10 km. In most of the main Spanish urban areas (Madrid, Barcelona, Valencia) this increase in temperatures has been permanently consolidated in recent years, in the range of two or three degrees Celsius (CIESIN, 2016).

The team of architects at RCR, winners of the Pritzker Architecture Prize in 2017, who were recently commissioned to remodel the Plaça dels Països Catalans, will have the opportunity to demonstrate how architecture and urban planning can respond to climate challenge while improving the social perception of the square.

Renovation Project for the Monument to the Fallen (Pamplona)

In January 2019, we submitted a proposal to the international ideas competition organized by the Pamplona City Council to modify the uses and redevelop the Monument to the Fallen and its surrounding urban area, which includes the Plaza de la Libertad, Serapio Esparza Park and the adjacent streets. Our proposal aimed to turn the area into a showcase for the ecological wealth of present-day Navarre and, ultimately, the testimony to a social pact for its future conservation. The decisions regarding the Monument to the Fallen have been fodder for intense political controversy. Some are in favor of maintaining the monument but giving it a new use and resignifying it – in other words, ensuring that its symbols and messages do not endorse, at any point, the superiority of the winning side. There have also been voices in favor of demolition. The controversy was stoked by the Navarra Administrative Court (TAN), which voided the jury's decision, and the City Council's subsequent decision to appeal the court's ruling.

Although our proposal was not selected, we still stand by the decision, especially from the standpoint of care, to allocate a large portion of the budget to the redevelopment of the surroundings, placing priority on the construction of public space, and making biodiversity the leitmotif in a new social and political accord. The notion that preserving environmental wealth should serve as the basis for a generalized social agreement was introduced in 1990 by Michel Serres, with great perspicacity, in his book *The Natural Contract*. The thesis is that the violence that humanity can exert on nature is will be answered by the Earth in kind, and that our survival depends on finding a regime of coexistence, a contract shared by all, that limits this mutual damage. The book by Serres was published before the evidence of the climate emergency, and its repeated denial, showed us that, broadly speaking, conservatives place less

Monument to the Fallen (Pamplona). Axonometric drawing of the whole.
©Izaskun Chinchilla Architects.

importance on environmental values than progressives (Nawrotzki, 2012). But we believe that his text can be held up as a foundation for trans-ideological political agreement – also because the sentiment varies by country and, for example, is different depending on the interpretation of local history: conservatives in communist countries are environmentalists and appreciate the environment as a safeguard of national values (Nawrotzki, 2012). Defending Serres' proposal would prevent environmental policies from being promoted from an exclusively progressive perspective, supporting a return to the idea of a pact, which allows conservatives to back environmental preservation without the feeling of having been singled out or attacked beforehand.

We should also recall that there are a limited number of places that can support biodiversity in the city. These include remnants of the natural landscape that may have been preserved within cities: vacant lots, which, in many cases, can only be of use temporarily; public parks and gardens; private gardens and courtyards, some balconies, and certain green roofs (Aronson et al., 2017).

Additionally, certain parameters must be met in order for this limited set of spaces in a city to form an effective support for biodiversity: size, quality, pattern, connectivity and diversity are some of them.[28] Size is one of the most critical aspects. The fragmentation and isolation of urban green spaces has been well defined in the UK, where it is estimated that only 13% of urban trees are found in green spaces larger than 0.25 hectares (Evans, Newston and Gaston, 2009). This statistical average contrasts with the indication that only areas between 10 and 35 hectares are capable, on their own, of providing support to urban species (both those that use them temporarily and their permanent inhabitants).

When there are no large natural spaces, anywhere between 10 and 35 hectares, across a large stretch of the city, support can only be provided by a network of smaller spaces, and in those cases their size and proximity are crucial. The decision to opt for paved squares means depriving urban centers of more than two hectares (in the case of the Plaça dels Països Catalans Square), or one hectare (Plaza de la Encarnación in Seville), in places where support for biodiversity depends on the construction of a network that is normally lacking in nodes. In areas such as the Centro district in Madrid, only the area formed by all the squares together, including Plaza de Callao (0.5 ha), Puerta del Sol (1.2 ha), Plaza de Santo Domingo (0. 35 ha) and Plaza Mayor (1.2 ha), among others, could begin to approach the construction of an effective support for biodiversity.

In the city, especially from the perspective of care, squares, corners, monuments or green spaces aren't just singular elements; they are

28 https://academic.oup.com/bioscience/article/67/9/799/4056044

part of a network that has the potential to contribute to preserving collective health and the environment. The open spaces of the city, seen from a perspective that supports urban biodiversity, should form part of a matrix structure in which these "urban patches" become the nodes in a network (Breuste et al., 2008; Wu, 2008). The strategy is to generate a mesh with the largest possible number of intersections and to articulate them through relations of proximity and diversity. For this to happen, there has to be a change in our vision of the city: understanding the pattern formed by the different elements beyond the nature of each individual piece. A good example of the need for a change in how we observe and analyze the city is the recent media controversy about whether the upcoming reform of the Puerta del Sol in Madrid should incorporate trees. The arguments cited the need to hold events and the importance of being able to view the complete façades in a historical setting. Some even blamed the architects, not entirely without reason, for lacking knowledge of landscape architecture. But among all these reasons, it did not occur to anyone to calculate the distance to the next shaded space, green space and fountain, and whether those spaces already formed a dense pattern, or if their continuity depended on the Puerta del Sol. The survival, or at least the minimum comfort, of many species in the city – among which I would include members of the population with difficulties related to age, health or economic purchasing power – depends biologically on the strength of that network.

In our proposal to renovate the urban area around the Monument to the Fallen in Navarra, this matrix structure was achieved through a series of landscape strips. Adapting to the pre-existing conditions, these strips occupied swaths between 2.5 meters and 9.5 meters wide, and ran through the site with interruptions, but made it possible for any flying species within the compact area of the square – for example, birds or insects – to encounter diverse habitats and plant species within a few meters.

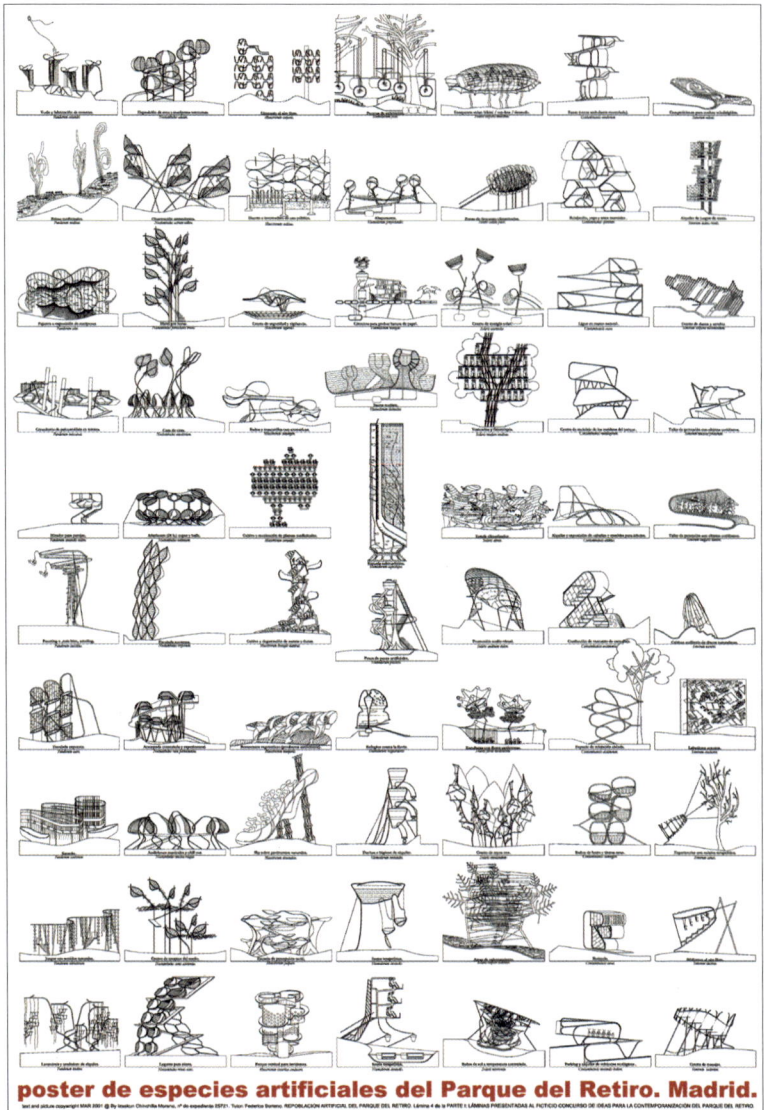

poster de especies artificiales del Parque del Retiro. Madrid.

Final Year Project. Poster of artificial species in the Retiro Park.
©Izaskun Chinchilla Moreno.

Monument to the Fallen (Pamplona).
Axonometric drawing, detail of ferns in Leitzalarrea.
©Izaskun Chinchilla Architects.

Our predilection for working on rehabilitation projects has led us to adopt different strategies to make biodiversity compatible with pre-existing conditions. In my final year project, *The Artificial Repopulation of the Retiro Park*, which involved working in a highly consolidated environment, new species and new natural habitats were introduced in a serious of isolated instances. At all times, however, each small intervention was considered an elements in the matrix, ensuring that the maximum distance to the next point did not exceed 20 meters. In a case like the Retiro project, where the intervention was centered on isolated points, additional elements are used provide continuity between the nodes, taking the place of the strips in the Navarre project, outlining connection corridors that can be reinforced in stages.

We might distinguish between two types of strategies in introducing biodiversity into the city: the implementation of corridors and the

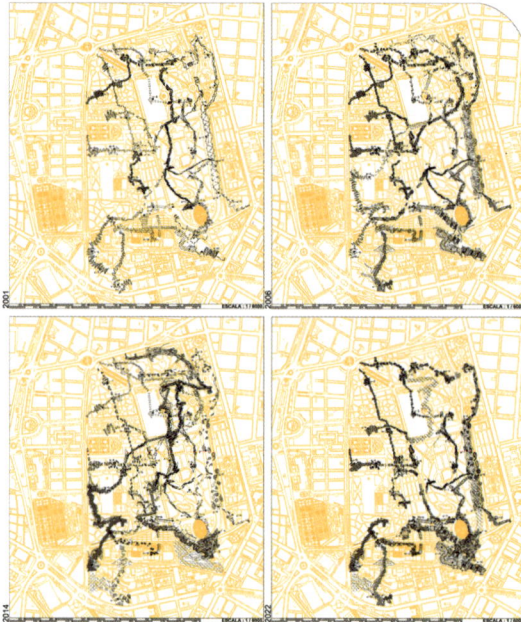

Final Year Project. General Plans. Evolution of
the project 2001-2022.
©Izaskun Chinchilla Moreno.

introduction of "stepping stones". Although the option of corridors
has proven to be extremely effective (Benide et al., 2015), the pre-
existing conditions in consolidated cities can make this difficult.
The introduction of stepping stones of biodiversity, like the stones
you might jump on as you cross a river, has also shown its potential
(Rudd et al., 2002), and it is often the only possible option. These
two variants often occur on different scales: on a territorial scale,
a corridor for biodiversity might be the Manzanares Linear Park,
which covers more than 97 hectares in its first section, and which is
still expanding in Madrid with section 2 (250 ha), and the complete
set of Madrid city parks function as islands. These strategies can

also be operational on the district level, implementing corridors when they are compatible with pre-existing conditions, or stepping stones when the former are not possible. Even on the scale of an urban intervention, like a square, these two logics can be effective in support of biodiversity. The important thing is not to lose sight of the larger matrix logic: the individual elements are not the only things that matter; the connectivity between them, the distance and continuity are also key.

Heterogeneity is another key aspect in the design of biodiverse urban spaces. Many species require different natural spaces for their survival. The seasons mark an important difference in the needs of living beings: in summer they may need shade and humidity, and in winter just the opposite. These different needs also affect animal species throughout their different life stages. If we generate heterogeneous environments, living beings can patch together an existence, according to their needs, by using the different environments at different times. I'd like to emphasize that, in this respect, a strategy that is good for bees, sparrows, or squirrels is equally good for human beings, with variable needs according to the season and stage of life.

Architects have been educated to homogenize the environment, because, among other reasons, from the point of view of the designer, the process is much more "economical" (I come up with a solution I like and repeat it) when compared to a commitment to heterogeneity (not only do I have to come up with several solutions but also deal with the problems that arise when I mix them together). Pursuing heterogeneity makes it worthwhile to identify a source, an origin that helps you understand, as a designer, which differences are relevant to you. In the case of the Retiro park, the columns in the matrix were given over to one of the positive effects of trees on the urban environment, contrasting with the rows that pursued heterogeneity in terms of social uses.

Monument to the Fallen (Pamplona).
Axonometric detail of the Irati Forest.
©Izaskun Chinchilla Architects.

In the case of the intervention in Pamplona, the heterogeneity came from trying to emulate some of the region's landscapes. The high biodiversity in Navarra is partly the result of its unusual location – at the confluence of three regions: Alpine, Atlantic and Mediterranean – and low population density (59 inhabitants per km^2, compared to 91 in Spain as a whole). Each strip pays homage to one of the characteristic forests or landscapes of the Navarre region, inviting visitors to travel metaphorically, without leaving Pamplona, to learn about them. The intervention could thus contribute to the economic and ecological vitality of the region, while promoting responsible internal tourism with a green intent.

Naturally, there are specific conditions of each ecosystem that cannot be replicated in the city (altitude, soil composition, proximity to a river or mountains). But there are other aspects that can be brought into urban spaces. Following are several examples.

- The combination of beech and fir trees of a certain size with hedges and a topographic construction made with wooden ribs to keep off the weather could spark curiosity about the species in the Irati Forest and its ground conditions, with a sloping terrain due to its location in the Pyrenees and painted with the rich colors of fallen leaves in autumn.

- The inclusion of productive gardens and greenhouse rental areas would make it possible to grow all kinds of vegetables, such as artichokes, asparagus, cardoons, lettuce hearts, spinach, borage, piquillo peppers, etc. inviting people to learn more about the areas of the region where the Ebro River makes Navarra into an extraordinarily fertile terrain.

- Taking advantage of the presence of areas that remain shaded for extended periods of long time and ensuring the preservation of the natural runoff from the terrain, it was possible to introduce fern plantations into the urban environment, recalling landscapes like Leitzalarrea.

- Oaks have shown excellent resilience to climate change and have become well-established urban trees in cities like New Orleans, Edinburgh and Washington D.C.; planting them in Pamplona could help us pay homage to the Orgi oak grove. We introduced a cobblestone pavement between the oaks, which, in addition to allowing natural runoff, reproduced motifs from the tree bark.

- New bio-construction solutions, such as geocells, make it possible to build a permeable base for the growth of grasses of different species, and their combination with mineral soils and sand, with a natural consolidated appearance and guaranteeing good drainage, offering excellent opportunities for picnics and enjoying outdoor cinema and inviting visitors to get to know the grasslands of Urbasa-Andia, a natural park between the Atlantic shore of Navarra and the Mediterranean.

Monument to the Fallen (Pamplona).
Axonometric detail of the Orgi oak grove.
©Izaskun Chinchilla Architects.

Monument to the Fallen (Pamplona).
Axonometric detail, Bertiz Lordship Natural Park.
©Izaskun Chinchilla Architects.

- The Bertiz Lordship Natural Park combines lavish forests with a botanical garden. In our tribute, we wanted to highlight their contribution to biodiversity by combining a large number of tree and shrub species in one strip. Using partially recycled bricks and pressed mineral soils, this strip additionally offered a shaded area based on an organic pattern.

These projects are intended to show ways of incorporating biodiversity into the city by slightly changing the tendency toward what we might call the culture of hard surfaces. City Council members and architects of a certain age have systematically positioned themselves in favor of "cleaner solutions", as defined by the current mayor of Madrid, Martínez Almeida, for the solution to redevelop the Puerta del Sol, which is so extreme that it is entirely devoid of vegetation, and which was the result of a competition organized by the Architects' Association of Madrid in 2014, won by Linazasoro & Sánchez Arquitectura. Architects and mayors use arguments like the preservation of historical heritage, but we have to remember that Madrid's Plaza Mayor, like so many others, had trees and fountains in it until 1927. Citizens should protest against the implementation of a paved square because it represents an irreplaceable loss for their health and wellbeing and for the survival of living species in the city. The historical or technical arguments (the existence of underground structures) are all questionable and can be managed, in all cases. The only compelling reasons to prioritize a paved square involve, once again, prioritizing productive activities (cleaning, security, control of public order, advertising, commerce, and the organization of for-profit events) above care for the environment and people's health – a formula that this book is intent on proving wrong – and, to look at it an even more perverse light, to preserve a visual culture of order and cleanliness that helps architects educated in the modern movement to differentiate their aesthetic preferences from those of everyday people.

Afterword

Preamble to a Declaration
of the Rights of City-Dwellers

AFTERWORD: PREAMBLE TO A DECLARATION OF THE RIGHTS OF CITY-DWELLERS

The two most famous and fundamental declarations of rights are the Universal Declaration of Human Rights, from 1948, and the Declaration of the Rights of the Child from 1959, based on the Geneva Declaration of 1924, both promoted by the UN. Like many other precedents which this text takes into account, there were many women who participated in their drafting, playing an essential role (Adami 2020). Considering the period in question, I would say there were probably more women present than would have been likely at any other UN event or any other institutional activity. The contribution of Eleanor Roosevelt, who essentially led the drafting of the declarations after the world wars, is perhaps the best known, but other women from more varied geographical origins also played fundamental roles – including Hansa Mehta from India and Minerva Bernadino from the Dominican Republic, who were responsible for the change in wording from "all men" to "all human beings" and for the explicit recognition of the equality of men and women in the preamble.

No doubt, bills of rights are one of the best ways to institutionalize care, so it is not surprising that women played a greater weight in their writing than in other efforts. In today's context, I think it would be important to collectively draft a Declaration of Rights of the Inhabitants of the City. The singular consequences of climate change and COVID-19 for those of us who live in urban environments have made this objective opportune, relevant, and even urgent. Moreover, the growing economic exploitation of shared spaces, which I mentioned when talking about POPS (privately owned public spaces) or the rising imposition of uniform lifestyles, which I associated with the concept of teleocracy, and the invisible associations between those principles and many smart city projects, all support the demand for collectively drafting that bill of rights.

Those rights should include the right to climate hope, to ecological mobility, the right to clean air and equal access to natural resources, the right to rest, to play and to leisure, and the right to intuition and to full cognitive development, which I have tried to anticipate in this book. No doubt we all believe that the definitive formulation of these points should be informed and supervised by committees of experts and, as I have said, it would be collective in nature. So, in this epilogue, I have preferred to write a preamble, a reflection on the wording of that possible declaration, with a focus on one specific aspect: the importance of ordinary citizens being a part of those commissions and the construction of their rights to participation and representation during the planning of the city and during its use. I believe that this cross-cutting methodological aspect would fundamentally affect the tone of each point. It also summarizes why care is so difficult to characterize institutionally: its organization and understanding can only come from experience and not from deduction.

Declarations of rights can also have a discouraging effect. Seven decades after the declaration, in 1948, that all human beings are born free and equal, we see how far off that ideal still is, which can lead to a lot of frustration. In consequence, in this epilogue, in addition to outlining a series of citizens' rights, I wanted to talk about the obligations of the public institutions and teams of experts that contribute to the construction of the city, albeit making reference only to partial aspects. In my professional experience, this is a step that we women especially, as a collective, need to take, which is still pending. We have been able to lay out the horizon we wish to reach, but, beyond that, we have to assert our right not to accept inherited norms and assume our responsibility to proactively change what is keeping us from our goal, even if it has a profound impact on the structure of professions, disciplines or social roles.

The right to understand and contribute to the construction of the empirical evidence that should be used to design the city

The diversity of the city's inhabitants is extraordinary and constitutes a fundamental value that must be preserved and encouraged. There are citizens of different ages, physical and mental conditions; diverse cultural backgrounds and customs; different sexual orientations; and different structures of cohabitation, among many other divergences. If we broaden our perspective even further, the diversity is even greater: we coexist with any number of other species.

City planning has been one of the areas of human activity in which technocratic principles have been most commonly applied. The implementation of planning methods based, a priori, on scientific principles to improve efficiency, competitiveness or profit have led to an overrepresentation of certain groups, generally coinciding with the profile of the people in charge of planning (heterosexual men of working age with a technical, business or university education), thus introducing a bias, significant inequalities, and a loss of opportunity for others.

Technocracy has also operated under the premise that the future of the city, and the future events that might affect it, can be predicted by science. Events that have been taking place since the 1970s, such as the increase in crime in residential neighborhoods with open blocks, planned as oases of coexistence, or, more recently, climate change and the unforeseen effects of growing environmental vulnerability and COVID-19, must reject this belief and consolidate an international consensus to plan for resilience, precisely, in the face of what we cannot foresee.

The city, therefore, should not be planned exclusively or fundamentally based on pre-established principles (of which, it is assumed, that technical teams have greater knowledge) but should take into account the empirical observations of how the different decisions affect the inhabitants: a process in which both experts and citizens are observers in real time, with nearly equal standing. In this construction of empirical evidence, the proactive participation of all sectors of society is essential, – first of all, because it is difficult to anticipate the effect of urban policies on an extraordinarily varied population base. One example is that shared space has contributed to reducing accidents, improving environmental quality and increasing the economic profitability of certain businesses on the street, but doesn't it also reduce the independence of children, the elderly or people with a visual impairment? There are design formulas that might alleviate these unwanted effects, but to achieve that, we need to be able to detect them in time – for example, if during the design process an urban area has been prototyped and examined extensively by a diverse group of citizens who have been given active assessment tools. Diversity is less predictable than normativity and, therefore, designing for diversity entails the defense of a careful and non-a priori empirical observation.

The need for building up a body of participatory empirical knowledge also has to do with the multifactorial aspect of the urban values we hope to construct: a low-density urban area may be fantastic for the preservation of biodiversity, but at the same time it may be very dependent on fossil fuels and contribute to segregating gender roles. As, as a society, when we diversify the criteria for measuring how good a city is, the unpredictable effects of urban policies, the kind that only emerge when "trying something out" or "watching and waiting", become more relevant.

The right to sovereignty over one's own actions and over the objects that condition them

We have seen how, in the examples of shared space inspired by Hans Monderman, both pedestrians and drivers maintain conscious sovereignty over their own actions. The absence of traffic signs makes drivers feel that they are invading the territory of the natural user of the city – the pedestrian – and, therefore, they are aware of the presence of a risk, which they need to assume and manage. Drivers are likely to slow down and pay more attention. The same happens with pedestrians: the absence of crosswalks and separate lanes for cars makes them aware that there is a risk they have to manage. From time to time, a vehicle could invade the space normally reserved for their use. Pedestrians and drivers are sovereign: they manage their own risks. The same thing happens when a child is climbing a tree in a forest or when we allow citizens to borrow folding chairs and set them up in their favorite spot in a public space.

Traffic signs, in conventional mobility spaces, "take away" sovereignty from pedestrians and drivers. Drivers perceive that they are moving through a space that is reserved for them, where pedestrians or cyclists are unauthorized invaders. Someone else has determined the speed, the rules, the code of conduct for them, and, therefore, they are less "careful". Being careful, paying attention to the needs of others, requires having sovereignty over one's own actions; the feeling of risk is a prior and necessary step for the conscious construction of the sense of co-responsibility. School playgrounds take away part of the sovereignty of play from children and interrupt the innate sense of co-responsibility towards the family group, because playgrounds are designed so that parents can only watch and wait. Bollards or benches that are fixed in single positions are examples of objects that limit sovereignty.

The gravest thing about this decline in citizen sovereignty, sometimes engendered by regulations or by codes of conduct, but ultimately materialized by objects, is that it is carried out, de facto, without prior political and social debate and without our being aware that it forces us to live under premises that are deeply influenced by ideologies we never accepted. So-called "hostile architecture" is, directly, a planned aggression against a group of vulnerable citizens that, in turn, limits the right of all the city's inhabitants, and which, historically, takes place in privately owned public spaces as a clear expression of a neoliberal ideology where the exploitation of space for commercial use is treated as a priority.

We need to find the formula for practical management in keeping with Latour's classic goal "to build the Parliament of Things" (Latour, 1993). For the caring city to exist, citizens must have the right to be consulted about the installation of objects in public space, which, in many cases, will be paid for by their taxes. Before the installation of smart streetlights (which may prioritize the most commercial neighborhoods), landscaping elements (which may serve to control traffic but can also be an obstacle for strollers) or advertisements, citizens should be given complete, transparent and reliable information about the objectives being pursued, and they must be able to voice their opinions, offer recommendations, exercise their right to veto and modification. The Netherlands, the Scandinavian countries and South Korea have chosen to impose mandatory consultancies in many urban regeneration processes (Jin et al., 2018).

Thre right to access and exercise active, inclusive and well-planned governance

Traditionally, planning has been seen as the action with the most influence over the construction of a city. Once it was completed, the work of architects, urbanists, politicians and planners was seen as finished, or moving into a secondary role. But the city is inhabited, traversed, exploited, bought, sold, rented, cared for, maintained, promoted, taught, discovered, rehabilitated, repaired, segregated, etc. The idea that politicians' and experts' work is done once the city is planned and built is equivalent to thinking that a doctor's work is over when someone is born.

With the example of mobility on demand, we have seen that governance can play a fundamental role in the final use that is given to public space. It is worth delving deeper into the type of governance that can encourage and support activities related to care.

Active governance. Governance takes place, de facto, in all the cities of the world. They all have town halls and urban police forces and the majority have municipal landscaping services, all of them with many tasks to perform. But there is a difference between whether the function of the local police is to ensure compliance with the law or, for example, to organize the transformation of a wide street into an area for playing, walking or riding bikes. Active governance is not limited to monitoring compliance with regulations and the correct and predictable functioning of resources; rather, it puts forward an agenda to improve the city and commits to improving the inhabitants' quality of life through the promotion of activities. Active governance is based on the premise that no city offers optimal support for the lives of all its inhabitants, and that it is possible to contribute to well-being by promoting new forms of collective use.

Inclusive governance. The planning of governance should, of course, account for the diversity to which we alluded in the previous section and foster the coexistence of diverse forms of life.

Governance should be planned and integrated as an unfinished and open dimension of infrastructure. Using the example of the bike path in Bogotá, we can delve into the advantages of planned governance. Any street or road can be adapted to an alternative use, other than the one it was originally planned for, through an action of governance: in the case of Bogotá, a total of 127.69 km of roads normally reserved for vehicle traffic are filled with bicycles every Sunday and holiday, from 7 a.m. to 2 a.m. the next day. This began in an unplanned way between 1974 and 1976, when residents demanded this use for certain roads; they succeeded in formalizing and institutionalizing the proposal in 1976. The program began to operate in a more planned way in 1995, when it was taken over by the Secretariat of Transit and the District Institute of Sports and Recreation (IDRD for its initials in Spanish): the advantage of incorporating planning is that the bike path program can also be oriented toward promoting social equality, by coordinating with other actions. Under the administrations of mayors Mockus and Peñalosa, this governance action, based on transforming an infrastructure designed for one use through temporary actions and administrative and citizen decisions, grew from 20 km to 120, introducing a night schedule and combining with "recreovías", streets allocated for aerobic exercise classes. As I see it, the example that most clearly shows the benefits of designing a city with the assumption that actions of governance will later be carried out is the coordination with the TransMilenio, Bogotá's transportation system consisting of above-ground buses that circulate in segregated lanes and which are accessed via a raised platform. The streets that were planned to shift their uses under the Mockus and Peñalosa administrations incorporated flexibility into their planning: the center lanes are always open to public transportation, and the outside lanes can be allocated for vehicles, bicycles, for pedestrian use, or civic uses. Through our à la carte mobility proposal and our defense of the theory of loose parts in the city, we invite urban planners, architects and municipal managers to imagine flexible, open and conceptually incomplete infrastructures, which require actions of governance to determine their final content, changing and adapted to the needs and desires of the city's residents.

The obligations of public entities: combining economic, environmental and health-related objectives

Are the policies that protect the environment and individual and collective health, and that promote and support care, necessarily wasteful and at odds with economic benefit? During much of its beginnings and in its early development, ecological thought was presented as antagonistic to economic growth. The *Meadows Report*, from 1972, made this dichotomy official. Donella Meadows, along with 17 other professionals, posited a 100-year limit for the Earth to be outgrown assuming constant population and economic growth at levels similar to those at the time of writing. They also proposed a solution: reigning in economic and population growth by tending toward a state of equilibrium. This type of analysis has been reiterated by systematic authors with solid arguments for more than three decades and, although they have played a key role in raising awareness about the need to shift from extractive and cumulative economic systems to circular ones with less impact, they have also fed into the belief that, almost always, we must make a choice between preserving the environment, personal and family health or well-being, and accumulating wealth.

More recently, attempts have been made to sketch out horizons for the environment, the economy, and health and comprehensive care as mutually reconcilable goals. One of these frameworks worth noting is referred to by its authors as "green capital". Christian de

Perthuis and Pierre-André Jouvet have posited a certain compatibility between economic growth and ecological preservation so long as certain rules of the financial market are adjusted (Perthuis, 2015). The path to conciliation, according to these authors, is to recognize the services and values that we normally already derive from natural capital with no associated cost and to incorporate those values among the signals (prices, costs, investments) and the decisions that make up the market. For De Perthuis and Jouvet, if we introduce a new price that assigns value to carbon emissions and greenhouse gases, it can also become a factor for growth and job creation.

Their proposal consists of adding cost and benefit to the services we now derive from nature, taking them for granted, free of charge and, consequently, without valuing them. There are currently some services that come from nature to which the market has assigned a price: for example, harvesting plants for food or for wood. But there are also services we take from nature without paying: most of the institutions that protect against flooding do not charge for the service, nor are we charged for clean air even when industry is a source of contamination, nor, in many parts of the world, is there a charge for the use of water or for dumping waste. The idea of green capital entails assigning a price and cost to all these services so that they become part of the cycles of growth.

The idea of assigning a financial value to what was previously free has also occurred in realm of care and has even been institutionalized. The International Monetary Fund has carried out several studies in which care is considered unpaid work, which is disproportionately laid on the shoulders of women and which, although it is often carried out voluntarily, is in many cases also perceived as something that leaves no room for choice due to cultural norms, gender roles in the labor market, and the lack of public services, infrastructure or policies for family support.[29] Although care has been correlated with unpaid work, the activities it entails are beginning to be characterized as an economic activity. For example, by measuring the activity in hours: women around the world perform an average of two hours a day of unpaid care work. Some arguments assert that this activity should be reflected in the GDP. In this way, the people who provide care in most cases – women – come to be understood as economic agents, recognizing that when women dedicate more time to care than men, it undermines their participation in the workforce and reduces the productivity of all economic activities.

In terms of health, there have also been many attempts to associate financial value with activities that were previously carried out for extra-economic reasons: such as valuing the savings that preventive medicine represents for health systems in financial terms. In fact, this message has been included in speeches by various candidates for president of the United States. Hillary Clinton, John Edwards, Mike Huckabee and Barack Obama used the argument that preventable causes of death such as smoking, an unhealthy diet, or a lack of physical exercise led to 900,000 deaths each year, 40% of all deaths in the United States, and that investing in prevention would save the national health system a lot of money (Cohen et al., 2008).

Giving financial and monetary value to care, to preventive health care, (for example, valuing not only the expense but also the savings it generates) or to the services we take from nature has an advantage that could be considered the starting point for a synchronization of financial and environmental objectives linked to health and care in our cities. But, before delving into the advantages of this action, it is worth asking who should be responsible for its execution: who can determine the value of clean air, or an hour of conversation that offers companionship to an elderly person who lives alone? Who has the ability to combine in a single price not only how much treatment to quit smoking should cost, but how much it will save

29 Reducing and Redistributing Unpaid Work: Stronger Policies to Support Gender Equality.

the health system subsequently? If we ask the economist Mariana Mazzucato, the answer is clear: the government. Mazzucato recalls that, when governments are aligned with innovation policies, they have an enormous capacity to develop dynamic data management capabilities by harnessing digital platforms and using them actively (Mazzucato, 2017).

A city council, for example, has a much greater ability to introduce a reduction of mobility in private vehicles associated with an increase in planting trees. It can engage in a multifactorial assessment of the potential benefits for sectors as varied as hospitality and preventive medicine, or with respect to parameters that can offer a quantitative analysis of social welfare in economic terms. COVID-19 has offered an excellent opportunity to determine the worth and the benefits of this multifactorial assessment: when attempts to revive the economy have been isolated from health and environmental considerations, they have ultimately proven ineffective. Cities are proof that this dependency always exists; the ability to detect it only depends on considering the right territorial and temporal frameworks – which systematically exceed four-year political mandates.

The State, on its different levels, could play a major role not only in the emerging "green technology" revolution, as Mazzucato asserts, but also in the construction of a value system – with a financial foundation and function – that strikes a balance between environmental and health objectives and a comprehensive understanding of care. This task of revealing the web of complexly interdependent costs and benefits must also protect the sovereignty of citizens and economic agents, providing them with a better foundation for their decision-making process.

The construction of these agendas, with a financial foundation, to coordinate different kinds of objectives can serve as the jumping off point for the revolution that needs to take place in our cities. But as Naredo points out in some of his writings (for example, Naredo, 2018), this conflation of value with monetary price, of wealth with money, has a perverse aspect: it perpetuates, almost unconsciously, a logic of unlimited growth, an extractive and accumulative human activity that uncritically repeats the models of the past. It invites us, in a way, to retain the same economic values, and to understand the world, once again, unidimensionally. Do we recall Marcuse's term from the beginning of this book? This starting point is thus insufficient – and even dangerous if it occurs in isolation. What other obligations can we identify?

The obligations of experts: Design as a support for life

Over the last two decades, media outlets have contributed to spreading the idea that something as simple as eating chicken instead of veal can contribute to cutting the carbon emissions associated with the food industry by 48%, almost in half. This finding contributed to a very significant increase, of 165%, in chicken consumption worldwide between 1990 and 2013, and 20% in China alone between 2011 and 2018 (Ritchie, 2017). But there is still a long way to go: replacing chicken with beans would reduce emissions 11 times more. Poultry farming has been called into question for its working conditions, and reducing the consumption of foods that use antibiotics in their production may become a priority for public health systems in many parts of the world.

But the proposal of eating chicken instead of veal, accompanied by truthful and verifiable data, is a step in the right direction: without infringing on citizen sovereignty, it turns everyday actions into conscious decisions, and it helps people to imagine plausible alternative lifestyle scenarios. A further step might be, for example, using an app like Yuka, which tells consumers how healthy or harmful a food is based on its sugar content, energy value, saturated fat, protein, fiber content, additives and salt. But what would happen if Yuka also provided data on a food's environmental impact, on the working conditions of its producers, or its contribution to disease prevention?

This is the framework that should inform the work of experts: the challenges facing cities in terms of the environment, health, and the recognition and integration of care cannot be addressed successfully without a significant transformation of our way of life. In my doctoral dissertation I referred to an "ecological revolution" that "changes everything", paraphrasing Naomi Klein (2014). In this lifestyle shift, it is fundamental not to usurp citizens' sovereignty over their own actions. The task of experts is to illustrate the alternative forms of life and offer a transparent evaluation of their advantages.

How does this translate into architecture and urban design? Architects can present models of zero-energy buildings or propose urban regeneration interventions so that a bedroom community will eventually have a good supply of jobs and facilities, and so that residents can satisfy all their daily needs within the radius of a 15-minute walk; we can design biodiverse squares or urban furniture that lets people choose where they want to sit. I think this book offers enough examples of the possibilities. We can also help highlight the advantages of these new ways of life over others, so citizens can select, transform, combine and develop the options that we have put together.

This work is not fundamentally compositional or geometric: the argument for determining whether a project is desirable, in keeping with this perspective of professional ethics, is not whether "it creates a clean image." Instead, it is whether it has a verifiable positive effect on the lives of a diverse population under continuous transformation. An improvement in quality of life that is posited as an offer, and which users can choose freely and critically. With stubborn frequency, architecture and urban planning have been practiced with the despotism of those who believe they have information and capabilities that others do not. The shift toward the caring city can only have one fundamental actor: its inhabitants. It is not enough for us to attempt to convince, force or educate a portion of the population to travel by subway or to introduce an equitable gender distribution in the responsibility for reproductive tasks. They have valuable information that we do not possess: the details of their lives, their emotions, their bodies, their habits and preferences. They must be the ones to choose among these multiple options.

Scale is a fundamental aspect. Ecology or feminism are not cultural or philosophical products intended for an elite; they are efforts toward social improvement that only work when they benefit everyone. Providing flexible working hours doesn't just benefit mothers and children, it could also mean a single man has time to learn the piano or play golf and, according to all studies, it increases productivity. From the perspective of climate justice or gender, we can pursue an improvement to broader organizational conditions.

As a corollary, we can summarize the tasks of architects and urban planners as follows:

• The ultimate goal of our work is to improve the different living conditions of the inhabitants of the environment we are working in; we have a responsibility to all of them. Geometry, space, or formal purity are possible means, never the ends.

• We need to leave behind the old idea, instilled in us at architecture school, that we know more about the city than its inhabitants. They know more about the goal we are pursuing: what they need to improve their lives.

- We need to avoid stripping inhabitants of their sovereignty by making decisions that only they should be making. That gesture eliminates all risk – and, with it, any co-responsibility. Let's remember what shared space has taught us: that civic behavior is rooted in trust and autonomy.

- We need to be aware, at all times, of the multifactorial complexity of the city – in its current situation and in its future states; let's remember that, with all certainty, our actions will have unexpected collateral effects, some of which will be negative; and through design and strategic planning, let's provide reversible actions and alternative plans.

BIBLIOGRAPHY

Abellán Alarcón, Antonio and Chinchilla Moreno, Izaskun (2010): "Huerta Escalable", in José María Torres Nadal and Juan Antonio Sánchez Morales (coords.), *Tisspas: taller para la innovación social y el desarrollo de servicios y productos arquitectónicos sostenible. Workshop for social innovation and development of sustainable architectural services and products*, Murcia, Cendeac, Observatorio del Diseño y la Arquitectura (Región de Murcia), pp. 30-43.

Adami, Rebecca (2020): *Women and the Universal Declaration of Human Rights*, s.l., Routledge.

Aldgate, Jane (ed.) (2006): *The Developing World of the Child*, London, Philadelphia, Jessica Kingsley Publishers.

Alexander, Christopher (2015): *A City Is Not a Tree.*

Alexander, Ernest R.; Mazza, Luigi and Moroni, Stefano (2012): "Planning without Plans? Nomocracy or Teleocracy for Social-Spatial Ordering", *Progress in Planning*, 77, no. 2, February, pp. 37-87.

Alonso, Cristian et al. (2019): "Reducing and Redistributing Unpaid Work: Stronger Policies to Support Gender Equality", International Monetary Fund.

Amin, Ash (2008): "Collective Culture and Urban Public Space", *City*, 12, no. 1, April, pp. 5-24.

Ansell, Chris and Gash, Alison (2007): "Collaborative Governance in Theory and Prac- tice", *Journal of Public Administration Research and Theory*, 18, no. 4, October 17, pp. 543-71.

Applegarth, Michael (2006): *Leading Empowerment: A Practical Guide to Change*, Oxford, Chandos.

Aronson, Myla *et al.* (2017): "Biodiversity in the City: Key Challenges for Urban Green Space Management", *Frontiers in Ecology and the Environment*, 15, April 10.

Bachrach, Peter and Baratz, Morton S. (1963): "Decisions and Nondecisions: An Analytical Framework", *The American Political Science Review*, 57, no. 3, September. p. 632.

Basta, Claudia (2013): *Ethics, Design and Planning of the Built Environment*, New York, Springer.

Bastin, Jean-Francois *et al.* (2019): "The Global Tree Restoration Potential", *Science*, 365, no 6.448, July 5, pp. 76-79.

Beck, Ulrich (1992): *Risk Society: Towards a New Modernity*, Theory, Culture & Society, London, Newbury Park, California, Sage Publications.

Becker, Mary (1999): "Patriarchy and Inequality: Towards a Substantive Feminism", *University of Chicago Legal Forum*, vol. 1999, article 3.

Beninde, Joscha; Veith, Michael and Hochkirch, Axel (2015): "Biodiversity in Cities Needs Space: A Meta-Analysis of Factors Determining Intra-Urban Biodiversity Variation", edited by Nick Haddad, *Ecology Letters*, 18, no. 6, June, pp. 581-92.

Berlin, Isaiah (2000): *The Proper Study of Mankind: An Anthology of Essays*, 1, New York, Farrar, Straus and Giroux.

Berry, Wendell (1981): *The Gift of Good Land: Further Essays, Cultural and Agricultural*, Berkeley, Counterpoint.

Breuste, Jürgen; Niemelä, Jari and Snep, Robbert (2008): "Applying Landscape Ecological Principles in Urban

Environments", *Landscape Ecology*, 23, December 1, pp. 1139-1142.

Broadbent, Geoffrey; Bunt, Richard and Jencks, Charles (eds.) (1980): *Signs, Symbols, and Architecture*, Chichester, New York, Wiley.

Brundtland, Gro Harlem and Commission mondiale surl'environnement et le développement

(2014): *Notre avenir à tous.*

Carmona, Matthew (2014): "Re-theorising Contemporary Public Space: A New Narrative and a New Normative", *Journal of Urbanism: International Research on Placemaking and Urban Sustainability*, 8, December 17, pp. 1-33.

Carsten, Janet and Hugh-Jones, Stephen (eds.) (1995): *About the House: Lévi-Strauss and Beyond*, Cambridge, New York, Cambridge University Press.

Champlin, John R., (ed.) (2009): *Paradigms of Political Power*, New Brunswick, New Jersey, Aldine Transaction.

Chinchilla Moreno, Izaskun (2004): "Concursos. Nuevo Boulevard del Ensanche de Vallecas: Accésit", *Arquitectos: información del Consejo Superior de los Colegios de Ar- quitectos de España*, no. 171, p. 56.

— (2007): "Las Dehesillas-Espartalia. Contrato urbano vs. Contrato doméstico vs. Contrato del agua", *Arquitectos: información del Consejo Superior de los Colegios de Arquitectos de España*, ISSN 0214-1124, no. 181, pp. 69-74.

Chomsky, Noam (1976): *Studies on Semantics in Generative Grammar*, 3, The Hague, Mouton.

CIESIN (Center for International Earth Science Information Network) (2016):

"Global Urban Heat Island (UHI) Data Set, 2013", NASA Socioeconomic Data and Applications Center (SEDAC), Palisades, New York.

Cohen, Joshua T.; Neumann, Peter J. and Weinstein, Milton C. (2008): "Does Preventive Care Save Money? Health Economics and the Presidential Candidates", *New England Journal of Medicine*, 358, no. 7, February 14, pp. 661-63.

Cruz, Nuno F. da; Rode, Philipp and McQuarrie, Michael (2019): "New Urban Governance: A Review of Current Themes and Future Priorities", *Journal of Urban Affairs*, 41, no. 1, January 2, pp. 1-19.

Deperthuis, Christian and Jouvet Pierre-André (2015): *Green Capital: A New Perspective on Growth*, New York, Columbia University Press.

Delgado, Manuel (2015): *El espacio público como ideología*, Madrid, Los Libros de la Catarata.

Edmunds, David and Wollenberg, Eva (eds.) (2003): *Local Forest Management: The Impacts of Devolution Policies*, London, Sterling, Earthscan Publications Ltd.

Estevan, Antonio and Sanz, Alfonso (1996): *Hacia la reconversión ecológica del transporte en España*, Bilbao, Madrid, Bakeaz, Centro de Documentación y Estudios para la Paz; CC OO, Secretaría de Salud Laboral y Medio Ambiente; Los Libros de la Catarata.

Evans, Karl L.; Newson, Stuart E. and Gaston, Kevin J. (2009): "Habitat Influences on Urban Avian Assemblages", *Ibis*, 151, no. 1, January, pp. 19-39.

Flannigan, Caileigh and Dietze, Beverlie (2018): "Children, Outdoor Play, and Loose Parts", *Journal of Childhood Studies*, March 17, pp. 53-60.

Ford, Edward R. (2009): *Five Houses, Ten details*, New York, Princeton Architectural Press, first edition.

Gaviria, Mario (2011): *El buen salvaje: de urbanitas, campesinos y ecologistas varios*, Barcelona, El Viejo Topo.

Gehl, Jan (2011): *Life between Buildings: Using Public Space*, Washington, D.C., Island Press.

Gibson, Jenny Louise; Cornell, Megan and Gill, Tim (2017): "A Systematic Review of Research into the Impact of Loose Parts Play on Children's Cognitive, Social and Emotional Development", *School Mental Health*, 9, no. 4, December, pp. 295-309.

Giddens, Anthony (1999): "Risk and Responsibility", *Modern Law Review*, 62, no. 1, January, pp. 1-10.

— (2008): *The Consequences of Modernity*, Cambridge, Polity Press.

Gold, Seymour M. (1976): "Social Benefits of Trees in Urban Environments", *International Journal of Environmental Studies*, 10, no. 1, January, pp. 85-90.

Gregory, Richard Langton (2005): *Eye and Brain: The Psychology of Seeing*, Princeton, Princeton University Press, 5th edition.

Habermas, Jürgen (1999): *The Structural Transformation of the Public Sphere: An Inquiry into a Category of Bourgeois Society*, Cambridge, Mass., MIT Press.

Hamilton-Baillie, Ben (2008): "Towards Shared Space", *URBAN DESIGN International*, 13, no. 2, June, pp. 130-38.

Hillier, Bill and Hanson, Julienne (2005): *The Social Logic of Space*, Cambridge, Cambridge University Press.

Hoffman, David; Perillo, Patty; Hawthorne Calizo, Lee S.; Hadfield, Jordan and Lee, Diane M. (2005): "Engagement *versus* Participation: A Difference That Matters", *About Campus*, 10, no. 5, November, pp. 10-17.

Holmes, Malcolm J. (1989): *Somers Town: A Record of Change*, London, London Borough of Camden Libraries and Art Dept.

Howard, Ebenezer and Osborn, Frederic J. (2001): *Garden Cities of Tomorrow*, Cambridge, Mass., MIT Press.

involve.org (s. f.) "People and Participation", at http://www.involve.org.uk/wp-con tent/uploads/2011/03/People-and-Participation.pdf

Ives, Colta Feller; Clark, Cynthia and Walter, Emily (2018): *Public Parks, Private Gardens: Paris to Provence*, New York, The Metropolitan Museum of Art.

Jacobs, Jane (1992): *The Death and Life of Great American Cities*, New York, Vintage Books.

Jin, Eunae; Lee, Woojong and Kim, Danya (2018): "Does Resident Participation in an Urban Regeneration Project Improve Neighborhood Satisfaction: A Case Study of 'Amicho- jang' in Busan, South Korea", *Sustainability*, 10, no. 10, October 18, p. 3755.

Joyce, Rosemary A. and Gillespie, Susan D. (2000): *Beyond Kinship Social and Material Reproduction in House Societies*, Philadelphia, University of Pennsylvania Press, at http://public.eblib.com/choice/PublicFullRecord.aspx?p=4875937

Karndacharuk, Auttapone; Wilson, Douglas J. and Dunn, Roger (2014): "A Review of the Evolution of Shared (Street) Space Concepts in Urban Environments", *Transport Reviews*, 34, no. 2, March 4, pp. 190-220.

Kayden, Jerold S. (2000): *Privately Owned Public Space: The New York City Experience*, New York, John Wiley.

Klein, Naomi and Archer, Ellen (2014): *This Changes Everything*, sound recording, New York, Audioworks.

Lady Allen of Hurtwood (1971): *Planning for Play*, London, Thames and Hudson.

Langstraat, Florian and Van Melik, Rianne (2013): "Challenging the 'End of Public Space': A Comparative Analysis of Publicness in British and Dutch Urban Spaces", *Journal of Urban Design*, 18, no. 3, August, pp. 429-48.

Latour, Bruno (1993): *We Have Never Been Modern*, Cambridge, Mass., Harvard University Press.

— (2005): *Reassembling the Social: An Introduction to Actor-Network Teory*, Clarendon Lectures in Management Studies, Oxford, New York, Oxford University Press.

—(2008): "A Cautious Prometheus? A Few Steps Toward a Philosophy of Design (with Special Attention to Peter Sloterdijk)", Cornwall, at http://www.bruno-la-tour.fr/sites/default/files/112-DESIGN-CORNWALL-GB.pdf

Lawrence, Henry W. (1993): "The Greening of the Squares of London: Transformation of Urban Landscapes and Ideals", *Annals of the Association of American Geographers*, 83, no. 1, March, pp. 90-118.

López de Lucio, Ramón (2007): *Construir ciudad en la periferia: criterios de diseño para áreas residenciales sostenibles*, Madrid, Mairea Libros.

Lynch, Kevin (2005): *The Image of the City*, Nachdr Publication of the Joint Center for Urban Studies, Cambridge, Mass., MIT Press.

—(2018): *La imagen de la ciudad*, Barcelona, Gustavo Gili.

Marcuse, Herbert (n.d.): "Marxism and Feminism", at http://platypus1917.org/wp-content/uploads/archive/rgroups/2006-chicago/marcuse_marxismfemi-nism.pdf

Marcuse, Herbert (2002): *One-Dimensional Man: Studies in the Ideology of Advanced Industrial Society, Abingdon*, Routledge.

Martí Ciriquián, Pablo and Moreno Vicente, Elisa (2014): "La transformación urbana y territorial de la ciudad de Murcia y su entorno (1977-2010)", *Estudios Geográficos*, 75, no. 276, June 30, pp. 261-309.

Mazzucato, Mariana (2017): *El Estado emprendedor: Mitos del sector público frente al privado*, Barcelona, RBA.

Mckinnon, Catriona (2006): *Toleration: A Critical Introduction*, London, New York, Routledge, at http://public.eblib.com/choice/publicfullrecord.aspx?p=308552.

Meadows, Donella H. and Club of Rome (eds.) (1972): *The Limits to Growth: A report for the Club of Rome's Project on the Predicament of Mankind*, New York, Universe Books.

Messerschidt, James W. (2018): *Hegemonic Masculinity: Formulation, Reformulation, and Amplification*, Lanham, Rowman & Littlefield.

Mitchell, Don (2017): "People's Park Again: On the End and Ends of Public Space",

Environment and Planning A: Economy and Space, 49, no. 3, March, pp. 503-18.

Mitterauer, Michael and Sieder, Reinhard (1982): *The European Family: Patriarchy* to *Partnership from the Middle Ages to the Present*, Oxford, Blackwell.

Montaner, Josep Maria (ed.) (2013): *Reader modelo Barcelona, 1973-2013*, Barcelona, Comanegra.

Moody, Simon and Melia, Steve (2014): "Shared Space – Research, Policy and Problems", *Proceedings of the Institution of Civil Engineers – Transport*, 167, n. 6, November, pp. 384-92.

Moore, Robin C. (1989): "Playgrounds at the Crossroads", in Irwin Altman and Ervin H. Zube (eds.), *Public Places and Spaces*, Boston, Mass., Springer US, pp. 83-120.

Moore, Robin and Young, Donald (1978): "Childhood Outdoors: Toward a Social Ecology of the Landscape", in Irwin Altman and Joachim F. Wohlwill (eds.), *Children and the Environment*, Boston, Mass., Springer US, pp. 83-130.

Mullin, Amy (2006): "Parents and Children: An Alternative to Selfless and Unconditional Love", *Hypatia*, 21, no. 1, pp. 181-200.

Mullin, Amy and Canadian Society for Continental Philosophy (2007): "Giving as Well as Receiving: Love, Children, and Parents", *Symposium*, 11, no. 2, pp. 383-95.

Naredo, José Manuel (2018): "Orígenes y enfoques de la Economía Ecológica", *Gestión y Ambiente*, 21, no. 1, supl., October 23, pp. 35-48.

National Co-ordinating Centre for Public Engagement (n.d.): "What Is Public Engagement?", https://www.publicengagement.ac.uk/explore-it/what-public-en-gagement.

Nawrotzki, Raphael J. (2012): "The Politics of Environmental Concern: A Cross-National Analysis", *Organization & Environment*, 25, no. 3, September, pp. 286-307. Nes, Akkelies van (2008): "Measuring the Urban Private-Public Interface", pp. 389-98.

Nicholson, S. (1972): "The Theory of Loose Parts: An Important Principle For Design Methodology", *Studies in Design Education, Craft and Technology*, Open University Press 4 (2), pp. 5-14.

Norberg-Schulz, Christian (1980): *Genius Loci: Towards a Phenomenology of Architecture*, New York, Rizzoli.

O'Connor, M. R. (2019): *Wayfinding: The Science and Mystery of How Humans Navigate the World*, New York, St. Martin's Press, first edition.

O'Mara, S. M. (2019): *In Praise of Walking: The New Science of How We Walk and Why It's Good for Us*.

Olson, Burton K. (1980): "Children, Nature, and the Urban Environment Proceedings of a Symposium-Fair", *Journal of Leisure Research*, 12, no. 3, July, pp. 291-292. Oriol, Manuel (2011): *Filosofía de la inteligencia*, Madrid, Fundación Universitaria San Pablo-CEU.

Palermo, Pier Carlo and Ponzini, Davide (2015): *Place-making and Urban Development: New Challenges for Contemporary Planning and Design*, Regions and Cities, New York, Routledge, Taylor & Francis Group.

Powell, Ken et al. (1992): *Stansted: Norman Foster and the Architecture of Flight*, London, Fourth Estate, Wordsearch.

Rasmussen, Steen Eiler (1962): *Experiencing Architecture*, Cambridge, Mass., MIT Press.

Reed, Edward (1988): *James J. Gibson and the Psychology of Perception*, New Haven, Yale University Press.

Ribot, Jesse C. (2003): "Democratic Decentralization of Natural Resources", in Nicolas Van De Walle, Nicole Ball, and Vijaya Ramachandran (eds.), *Beyond Structural Adjustment*, New York, Palgrave Macmillan US, pp. 159-182.

Ritchie, Hannah (2017): "Meat and Dairy Production", *OurWorldInData.org*, at https://ourworldindata.org/meat-production

Roo, Gert de (2018): "Ordering Principles in a Dynamic World of Change – On Social Complexity, Transformation and the Conditions for Balancing Purposeful Interventions and Spontaneous Change", *Progress in Planning*, 125, October, pp. 1-32.

Rowe, Colin and Stutzky, Robert (1997): *Transparency*, Basil, Boston, Birkhäuser Verlag.

Rudd, Hillary; Vala, Jamie and Schaefer, Valentin (2002): "Importance of Backyard Habitat in a Comprehensive Biodiversity Conservation Strategy: A Connectivity Analysis of Urban Green Spaces", *Restoration Ecology*, 10, no. 2, June, pp. 368-75.

Sahuí, Alejandro (2002): *Razón y espacio público: Arendt, Habermas y Rawls*, México D.F., Coyoacán.

Schneekloth, Lynda H. and Shibley, Robert G. (1995): *Placemaking: The Art and Practice of Building Communities*, New York, Wiley.

Serrano Martínez, José Mª and García Marín, Ramón (2007): "La dimensión urbana en la ordenación del territorio regional: el ámbito metropolitano de Murcia. Aportaciones acerca de sus cambios recientes", *Estudios Románicos*, 17 (2), Universidad de Murcia, pp. 73-88.

Serres, Michel (1995): *The Natural Contract*, Studies in Literature and Science, Ann Arbor, University of Michigan Press.

Sikor, Thomas; He, Jun and Lestrelin, Guillaume (2017): "Property Rights Regimes and Natural Resources: A Conceptual Analysis Revisited", *World Development*, 93, May, pp. 337-349.

Sitte, Camillo and Stewart, Charles T. (2013): *The Art of Building Cities: City Building According to Its Artistic Fundamentals*, New York, Reinhold Publishing Corporation.

Solà-Morales, Ignasi de (2003): *Diferencias: topografía de la arquitectura contemporánea*, Barcelona, Gustavo Gili.

Still, Judith (1997): *Feminine Economies: Thinking against the Market in the Enlightenment and the Late Twentieth Century*, Manchester, Manchester University Press.

Temes Cordovez, Rafael *et al.* (2019): "Las Huertas periurbanas del mediterráneo (Murcia-Alicante-Valencia y Zaragoza). Primeros resultados de investigación para el caso de Valencia", III Congreso Internacional ISUF-H, CIUDAD COMPACTA VS. CIUDAD DIFUSA, editorial de la Universitat Politècnica de València.

Tonucci, Francesco (1998): *La ciudad de los niños: un modo nuevo de pensar la ciudad*, El árbol de la memoria, Madrid, Fundación Germán Sánchez Ruipérez, 2nd edition.

—(2015): *La ciudad de los niños*, Barcelona, Graó.

Van Kooten, G. Cornelis; Shaikh, Sabina Lee and Suchánek, Pavel (2002): "Mitigating Climate Change by Planting Trees: The

Transaction Costs Trap", *Land Economics*, 78, no. 4, November, pp. 559-72.

Voce, Adrian (2015): *Policy for Play: Responding to Children's Forgotten Right*, at http:// site.ebrary.com/id/11118311

Wang, Shugen (2002): "Framework of Pattern Recognition Model Based on the Cognitive Psychology", Geo-Spatial Information Science, 5, no. 2, January, pp. 74-78.

Ward, Kathrin; Lauf, Steffen; Kleinschmit, Birgit and Endlicher, Wilfried (2016): "Heat Waves and Urban Heat Islands in Europe: A Review of Relevant Drivers", *Science of The Total Environment*, 569-570, November 1, pp. 527-539.

Wolf, Kathleen L.; Lam, Sharon T.; McKeen, Jennifer K.; Richardson, Gregory R. A.; Van den Bosch, Matilda and Bardekjian, Adrina C. (2020): "Urban Trees and Human Health: A Scoping Review", *International Journal of Environmental Research and Public Health*, 17, no. 12, June 18, p. 4371.

Wu, Jianguo (2008): "Changing Perspectives on Biodiversity Conservation: From Species Protection to Regional Sustainability", *Biodiversity Science*, 16, no. 3, p. 205.

Zimmerman, Klaus and Bauer, Thomas (2002): *The Economics of Migration*.

IZASKUN CHINCHILLA

Architect, PhD, and professor of Architectural Practice at the Bartlett School of Architecture (London). She is one of the few women architects in Spain who runs her own architecture studio, Izaskun Chinchilla Architects. She has been named by the RIBA as an honorary fellow. She defends a staunch commitment to critical innovation for her profession, connecting architecture with ecology, sociology, and science.

The Caring City
HEALTH, ECONOMY AND ENVIRONMENT

Published by
Actar Publishers, New York, Barcelona
www.actar.com

Author/Editor
Izaskun Chinchilla Moreno

Translation
Angela Kay Bunning

Graphic Design
ACTAR

Printing and Binding
Arlequin, Barcelona

Distribution
Actar D, Inc. New York, Barcelona.

New York
440 Park Avenue South, 17th Floor
New York, NY 10016, USA
T+1 2129662207
salesnewyork@actar-d.com

Barcelona
Roca i Batlle 2
08023 Barcelona, Spain
T +34 933 282 183
eurosales@actar-d.com

Indexing
English ISBN: 978-1-63840-065-3
Library of Congress Control Number:
2022945429

Printed in Spain

Publication date
December 2022